Let's Learn German A2

Grammar and everyday spoken German for beginners

Gourav Vivek Kulkarni

NOTION PRESS

i

NOTION PRESS

India. Singapore. Malaysia.

ISBN xxx-x-xxxxx-xx-x

Contents

Preface

It gives immense happiness to meet you through this new book. It is always a pleasure to write and interact with all those who love to read and learn something new! This book thus comes as a continuation to the book titled 'Let's Learn German A1' by me, released last year.

Learning a foreign language is fun but writing a book on the same is quite challenging as every letter should be written with responsibility such that the reader gains competence as well as confidence during the process of learning. This book is thus a humble attempt to unfold the Grammar and certain exerpts of everyday spoken German of the A2 level of the CEFR. Once the user reaches the A2 level, simple day to day conversations can be easily carried out and one can get ready to move from the beginner stage (A1, A2) to the intermediate stage (B1, B2)

Similar to the way in which the contents of the book 'Let's Learn German A1' have been presented, this book also comes with a wide variety of examples in the form of sentences with every concept displayed in an attractive form for easy comprehension.

It is necessary to note that as higher levels are reached, one should start thinking in German and making sentences accordingly. The use of English has thus been done in this book only as a guide and the equivalent statements written should not be taken as direct translations.

The pattern of Goethe A2 Examination has also been explained as a chapter by itself. The Appendix portion can be called the 'Unique Selling Point' of this book as it contains a variety of consolidated data in the form of charts that can rarely be found in any other book to the tune of details as in this book. These charts serve as references to exercise the language and build competence for further levels.

By the time the reader completes reading this book, an ability to understand and reproduce German language equivalent to the A2 level of the Common European Framework of Reference (CEFR) of languages can be expected!

All the Best! – Alles Gute!

Gourav Vivek Kulkarni
(Exambekar)
B.E. (Mech)
Belagavi, Karnataka, India
gouravk36@gmail.com

10-Jan-22

The very intention behind writing this book was that it would reach German learning students, first time leaners and those intending to polish their German skills.

It was never even thought that within a period of three years of its release, this book would inch towards a wonderful milestone of sale of 1000 copies in paperback and would be accessed by thousands of readers and students worldwide!

My sincere thanks to all those who have learnt German using this book and I wish new lerners all the best !! Alles Gute !!

Gourav Vivek Kulkarni
(Exambekar)
BE (Mech), M.Tech (Machine Design)
Belagavi, Karnataka, India
1-Feb-2025

Acknowledgments

Every well accomplished task is incomplete without the mention of those minds and hands that have selflessly contributed to bring it to shape. I would hereby like to thank all those who have directly or indirectly contributed to bring this book to shape.

I thank my parents, Adv. Vivek G. Kulkarni (Exambekar) and Sou. Roopa V. Kulkarni (Exambekar) for their complete support and motivation to take up any task in life. Especially as it comes to learning of foreign languages, my father had motivated me to learn French during the days of Pre-University Course during 2011-2013 (PUC - Equivalent to 11th and 12th in Karnataka), by virtue of which today I can experience the world from many new dimensions!

During the days of graduation at KLS Gogte Institute of Technology, many of my friends used to attend German language classes. But one of them, Gaurang Kulkarni was the most dedicated towards learning the language. Many a times, when we used to be together, he used to mutter the German verb conjugations endlessly and that used to make me adore his zeal towards learning.

It was sometime in December 2020 that I started learning German by following an online course on German 1 by IIT Madras on the NPTEL Platform. One of our relatives, Dr. Inamdar had recommended this course as he was undergoing it himself. I casually opened it as it was freely available and then there was no looking back!

Dr. Milind Brahme and Dr. Sashirekha are my virtual teachers of German whom I haven't met personally but would like to meet one day and thank for their lectures in the NPTEL Course. Every lecture is a gem by itself and it is because of Dr. Brahme that I developed enormous interest in the language and was able to understand and frame sentences at length by the end if the course!

During the second wave of COVID-19 during May 2021, someone also suggested to learn German from videos of Mr. Kedar Jadhav on YouTube. The best thing of those videos was that I could learn German in my mother tongue Marathi and relate further with the grammar of the language! I also thank my friend Ranjit Desai for making it a point to text and chat in German so that I could get a good hold of the German slang as well.

In all German sentences, the most important information like the verb or the participle or the intonation is mentioned at the end. As rightly said by Mark Twain in his essay, 'The awful German language', that this is like an applause to all the preceding elements, I would like to mention my friend, Gouri S Killekar who is someone who deserves this position of applause in my German learning process. She has always been a guide during the learning process and is always available to answer my questions related to grammar and spoken German to this day!

My sincere thanks to all of you!

Vielen Dank!

1. Degrees of Comparison – Positiv, Komparativ und Superlativ

In spoken as well as written German, there are three degrees of comparison viz. Positiv (Positive), Komparativ (Comparative) and Superlativ (Superlative). It has been established that while learning new adjectives, one should always learn the antonyms as well as the forms of the degrees of comparison. This chapter shall elaborate the method of formation of the degrees of comparison and the way in which sentences can be formed to express preferences and opinions using the same. The examples mentioned for each degree are related to each other and a consolidated table at the end can help understand all the degrees at a glance.

1.1 Positive degree (Positiv)

The Positive degree is generally used to describe a noun. One may also use it to describe the state of the noun. This means that while using the Positive degree, one does not compare two or more objects and the discussion is limited to a single object. The nominative case is thus used to express the Positive degree.

While using the positive degree, the adjectives are written in their basic form and are generally placed at the end of the sentence. It is noteworthy that in German sentences, the most important information to be conveyed is written towards its end. Certain examples are as follows:

Sl. No.	Adjective	German Sentence	English equivalent
1	neu	Das Haus ist **neu**.	*The house is **new**.*
2	hell	Die Zimmer sind **hell**.	*The rooms are **bright**.*
3	schnell	Der Zug geht **schnell**.	*The train goes **fast**.*
4	kalt	Heute ist es **kalt**.	*It is **cold** today.*
5	gut	Mein Kuli schreibt **gut**.	*My pen writes **good**.*

There is another way in which one can express adjectives with feelings in the positive degree. This can be done by using the particles 'sehr' and 'zu'. The particle 'sehr' is used to indicate a positive intention like that of giving information while the particle 'zu' expresses a kind of negative intention or a feeling of discomfort. Both are explained as follows:

	German Sentence	Intention
sehr	Das Wetter heute ist **sehr** kalt.	*This is like saying the weather is 'very cold' and the person saying it is just giving information about it.*
zu	Das Wetter heute ist **zu** kalt.	*This is like saying the weather is 'too cold' and the person saying it is certainly feeling uncomfortable.*

1.2 Comparative degree (Komparativ)

The Comparative degree is used to compare two or more nouns. The way in which comparative degree of adjectives is written in German is same as that of English. An 'er' is added to the adjective as a suffix but there may be a few exceptions in case of irregular forms. The appendix sections in the book on German A1 and this book comprises of a comprehensive and elaborate list of degrees of comparison for various adjectives and their antonyms.

The Comparative degree can be used in two instances as follows.

1.2.1 To express: One of the nouns is superior or inferior as compared to the other

There are situations where we wish to express opinions or preferences regarding something compared to something else. The word 'als' is used to indicate that one of the nouns is superior or inferior compared to the other.

Sl. No.	Adjective	German Sentence	English equivalent
1	neu	Mein Haus ist **neuer als** sein Haus.	*My house is **newer than** his house.*
2	hell	Das Wohnzimmer ist **heller als** das Schlafzimmer.	*The living room is **brighter than** the bedroom.*
3	schnell	Das Flugzeug geht **schneller als** der Zug.	*The aeroplane goes **faster than** the train.*
4	kalt	Heute ist es **kälter als** gestern.	*It is **cooler** today **than** yesterday.*
5	gut	Ihr Kuli schreibt **besser als** mein Kuli.	*Her pen writes **better than** my pen.*

1.2.2 To express: The nouns are equally good or bad as each other

The phrase 'so … wie' is used to indicate that both the objects are comparable to each other. However, with a negation, the sentence can indicate preferences indirectly. In this type of expression, the adjective in its basic form is written between 'so' and 'wie'. The negation 'nicht' if used to indicate negation, is placed before 'so'.

Sl. No.	Adjective	German Sentence	English equivalent
1	neu	Mein Haus ist **so neu wie** sein Haus.	*My house is **as new as** his house.*
2	hell	Das Wohnzimmer ist **so hell wie** das Schlafzimmer.	*The living room is **as bright as** the bedroom.*
3	schnell	Der Zug geht **nicht so schnell wie** das Flugzeug.	*The train doesn't go **as fast as** the aeroplane.*
4	kalt	Heute ist es **so kalt wie** gestern.	*Today it is **as cold as** yesterday.*
5	gut	Ihr Kuli schreibt **nicht so gut wie** mein Kuli.	*Her pen doesn't write **as good as** my pen.*

1.3 Superlative degree (Superlativ)

The Superlative degree is used to express strong preferences wherein a noun is declared to be of the highest standing compared to all others put together. If negated, the sentences can convey a strong dislike. Superlatives are formed by adding '**sten**' as a suffix to the adjective and writing '**am**' before it.

z.B: **am** billig**sten**, **am** besten usw..

Certain examples are as follows:

Sl. No.	Adjective	German Sentence	English equivalent
1	neu	Das Haus ist **am neusten**.	*The house is **the newest**.*
2	hell	Dieses Zimmer ist **am hellsten**.	*This room is **the brightest**.*
3	schnell	Das Fahrrad geht nicht **am schnellsten**.	*The bicycle does not go **the fastest**.*
4	kalt	Heute ist es **am kältesten**.	*Today it is **the coldest**.*
5	gut	Mein Kuli schreibt **am besten**.	*My pen writes **the best**.*

Superlativ in adverbial sense ends with **–(s)ten**
z.B: Dieses Zimmer ist am hell**sten**.
This room is the brightest.

When used as an adjective, it ends with **–(s)te**. The ending may further vary depending on the case and other aspects which have been elaborated in the chapter on Adjektivdeklination.
z.B: Dieses Zimmer ist das hell**ste** Zimmer in unserem Haus.
This is the brightest room in our house.

It was seen that certain forms of adjectives in comparative and superlative degree have a change in vowel from a to ä or u to ü. There are certain irregular forms as well in which the words indicating higher degrees are completely different from the adjective. The following table provides a list of the positive, comparative, and superlative degrees for some adjectives. It may also be observed that the comparative and superlative degrees may have an umlaut included which is generally not considered irregular. The appendix sections in the book on German A1 and this book comprises of a comprehensive and elaborate list of degrees of comparison for various adjectives with their antonyms.

Adjektiv	Komparativ	Superlativ	Adjektiv	Komparativ	Superlativ
alt	älter	am ältesten	rot	röter	am rötesten
billig	billiger	am billigsten	schön	schöner	am schönsten
groß	größer	am größten	schwer	schwerer	am schwersten
hoch	höher	am höchsten	gern	lieber	am liebsten
jung	jünger	am jüngsten	gut	besser	am besten
kalt	kälter	am kältesten	viel	mehr	am meisten

Following table provides a consolidation indicating all the degrees of comparison for the adjective examples considered earlier.

Adjective	Degree	German Sentence
neu	Positiv	Das Haus ist **neu**.
	Komparativ 1	Mein Haus ist **neuer als** sein Haus.
	Komparativ 2	Mein Haus ist **so neu wie** sein Haus.
	Superlativ	Das Haus ist **am neusten**.
hell	Positiv	Die Zimmer sind **hell**.
	Komparativ 1	Das Wohnzimmer ist **heller als** das Schlafzimmer.
	Komparativ 2	Das Wohnzimmer ist **so hell wie** das Schlafzimmer.
	Superlativ	Dieses Zimmer ist **am hellsten**.
schnell	Positiv	Der Zug geht **schnell**.
	Komparativ 1	Das Flugzeug geht **schneller als** der Zug.
	Komparativ 2	Der Zug geht **nicht so schnell wie** das Flugzeug.
	Superlativ	Das Fahrrad geht nicht **am schnellsten**.
kalt	Positiv	Heute ist es **kalt**.
	Komparativ 1	Heute ist es **kälter als** gestern.
	Komparativ 2	Heute ist es **so kalt wie** gestern.
	Superlativ	Heute ist es **am kältesten**.
gut	Positiv	Mein Kuli schreibt **gut**.
	Komparativ 1	Ihr Kuli schreibt **besser als** mein Kuli.
	Komparativ 2	Ihr Kuli schreibt **nicht so gut wie** mein Kuli.
	Superlativ	Mein Kuli schreibt **am besten**.

2. Articles and Particles

2.1 Articles learnt at A1 level

All the basic types of articles have been learnt at the A1 level. These include Unbestimmterartikeln (indefinite articles), Bestimmterartikeln (definite articles), Negationartikeln (negation articles) and Possesivartikeln (posessive articles). There are various forms that these articles take according to the gender, number and case. These have been summarized as follows:

die Unbestimmterartikeln - Nominativ, Akkusativ und Dativ

	maskulin	feminin	neutrum	plural
Nominativ	ein	eine	ein	-
Akkusativ	einen	eine	ein	-
Dativ	einem	einer	einem	-

die Negationartikeln - Nominativ, Akkusativ und Dativ

	maskulin	feminin	neutrum	plural
Nominativ	kein	keine	kein	keine
Akkusativ	keinen	keine	kein	keine
Dativ	keinem	keiner	keinem	keinen

die Bestimmterartikeln - Nominativ, Akkusativ und Dativ

	maskulin	feminin	neutrum	plural
Nominativ	der	die	das	die
Akkusativ	den	die	das	die
Dativ	dem	der	dem	den

2.2 Possessive articles in Dative Case (Possessivartikeln im Dativ)

Possessive articles are used to indicate the possession of the noun. The forms of possessive articles in the Nominative and Accusative Case have been studied in detail at A1 level with examples. Following possessive article forms are used with the Dative case.

Pronomen	maskulin	feminin	neutrum	plural
ich	meinem	meiner	meinem	meinen
du	deinem	deiner	deinem	deinen
er	seinem	seiner	seinem	seinen
sie	ihrem	ihrer	ihrem	ihren
es	seinem	seiner	seinem	seinen
wir	unserem	unserer	unserem	unseren
ihr	eurem	eurer / euerer	eurem	euren / eueren
sie	ihrem	ihrer	ihrem	ihren
Sie	Ihrem	Ihrer	Ihrem	Ihren

The possessive articles in Dative case are accompanied by prepositions most of the times if not all the time. Some examples are as follows:

	Preposition	German sentence	English equivalent
ich	zu	Ich schreibe **zu meinem** Lehrer eine E-Mail.	*I am writing an E-mail to my Teacher.*
du	von	Du hast **von deiner** Freundin eine Einladung bekommen.	*You have received an invitation from your (girl)friend.*
er	nach	Er geht **nach seinem** Konzert ins Restaurant.	*He goes to the restaurant after his concert.*
sie	mit	Sie kommt morgen **mit ihren** Eltern.	*She is coming tomorrow with her parents.*
es	aus	Es ist **aus seinem** Haus hier gekommen.	*It has come out of its house here.*
wir	bei	Wir arbeiten **bei unserer** Firma in Belgaum.	*We work at our company in Belgaum.*
ihr	zu	Ihr gebt **zu euren** Kindern Schokolade.	*You give chocolates to your children.*
sie	von	Sie müssen **von ihrem** Chef Erlaubnis bitten.	*You have to request permission from your Boss.*
Sie	nach	Sie sind jetzt **nach Ihrem** Geburtsland gefahren.	*You have now driven to your country of birth.*

At times, these articles may be used to indicate the possession of the indirect object(s) in the sentence. In such cases, the Dative object is attached with the possessive article in Dative case. Some examples are as follows. For ease of understanding the same verb and nouns have been used with variations in the pronouns and corresponding dative possessive articles.

Pronomen	Aussagesätze
ich	**Ich** schreibe **meiner** Freundin eine Postkarte.
du	**Du** schreibst **deiner** Freundin eine Postkarte.
er	**Er** schreibt **seiner** Freundin eine Postkarte.
sie	**Sie** schreibt **ihrer** Freundin eine Postkarte.
es	**Es** schreibt **seiner** Freundin eine Postkarte.
wir	**Wir** schreiben **unserer** Freundin eine Postkarte.
ihr	**Ihr** schreibt **eurer** Freundin eine Postkarte.
sie	**Sie** schreiben **ihrer** Freundin eine Postkarte.
Sie	**Sie** schreiben **Ihrer** Freundin eine Postkarte.

Thus the inflexion of the possessive article depends on the gender, number and case of the noun whose possession has to be indicated.

2.3 Particles - denn, doch, gern(e), schon, sofort

Any language is made up of a certain building blocks. Some of them like nouns, verbs, adjectives and other parts of speech form the major blocks. But it is true that the blank space between the letters is as important as the letters themselves and so are certain particles required to add a flavour to the language. Particles are used more often in spoken language than written language to express emphasis. Five such particles shall be studied in this section.

2.3.1 denn

The particle **denn** is used to show interest and participation in a certain conversation. There may be certain situations wherein we may need to seek certain information from someone but asking it plainly might sound a bit rude. In such situations, this particle can make the conversation sound a bit polite and may show participative behaviour. Following examples explain the same [2]

		German Sentence	Significance
1	informell	Wie heißt du denn?	*At times if we meet someone in a Party or a function and after a considerable conversation, it may happen that we have not asked each other's name. In such situation, the particle **denn** doesn't make the other person feel offended on asking their name*
	formell	Wie heißen Sie denn?	
2	informell	Wann bist du denn hier gekommen?	*While asking about the arrival of guests, the particle **denn** can help one sound polite.*
	formell	Wann sind Sie denn hier gekommen?	
3	informell	Was machst du denn von Beruf?	*This particle can be useful while asking about professions. One can sound less interrogative by the use of **denn**. This helps avoid any kind of awkwardness.*
	formell	Was machen Sie denn von Beruf?	

The particle denn may kindly not be confused with the connector denn which has been discussed in the chapter on Sentence conectors.

2.3.2 doch

The particle **doch** is used to express a strong positive answer to a negative question. It may be used as a part of a sentence or all by itself. It is known from the study at the A1 level that <u>kein</u> is used to negate nouns or adjectives while <u>nicht</u> is used to negate verbs.

There may be situations where the person asking questions may ask a negative question. Negative question is asking something like, "Would you <u>not</u> like to eat now?" While answering such questions with a positive response, in German the particle **doch** can be used.

It is generally seen that this particle is used with the Ja/Nein Fragen. The Ja-Nein Fragen are of two types; one with a positive question and another with a negation in the question. To answer a positive question, one can simply reply with **Ja** or **Nein** whereas **Doch** is a particle used to reply to a negative question with a positive answer. Doch is also used to put emphasis. Following table presents certain examples using the two negating words <u>kein</u> and <u>nicht</u>. The table provides certain example sentences with their English equivalents written below.

		Fragen	**Antworten**	
1	Deutsch	Haben Sie heute Abend Zeit?	**Ja**. Ich habe viel Zeit für dich.	**Nein**. Es tut mir leid. Heute Abend habe ich keine Zeit.
	English	*Do you have time this evening?*	*Yes. I have a lot of time for you.*	*No. I'm sorry. I have no time this evening.*
2	Deutsch	Haben Sie heute Abend keine Zeit?	**Doch**. Ich habe viel Zeit für dich.	**Nein**. Es tut mir leid. Heute Abend habe ich keine Zeit.
	English	*Do you have <u>no</u> time this evening?*	*Certainly I do have a lot of time for you.*	*No. I'm sorry. I have no time this evening.*
3	Deutsch	Ich finde den Fisch so frisch. Oder?	**Ja** genau!	**Nein**. Ich finde ihn nicht so frisch.
	English	*I find the fish very fresh. What say?*	*Yes ofcourse!*	*No. I don't find it that fresh.*
4	Deutsch	Ich finde den Fisch so frisch. Er schmeckt dir nicht?	**Doch**. Ich finde ihn frisch auch!	**Nein**. Ich habe ihn nicht so frisch gefunden.
	English	*I find the find very fresh. Don't you like it?*	*Certainly I too find it fresh!*	*No. I haven't found it that fresh.*

Under the heading 'Antworten', the first column indicates a positive response whereas the second column indicates a negative response. It can be seen that when the question is positive as in Sl. nos. 1 and 3, the positive answer is simply "Ja" which may or may not be followed by a supporting sentence. But when the question is negative as in Sl. nos. 2 and 4, the positive answer is "Doch" which may or may not be followed by a supporting sentence. There is no such concept seen in English hence the English equivalents have been added with 'certainly' to compensate for the same.

As seen for all the questions, the second column under the heading 'Antworten' indicates a negative response. The way in which this response is given is the same irrespective whether the question is posed in a positive manner or a negative manner.

2.3.3 gern / gerne

The particle **gern / gerne** is used to express a general like or a preference. The reader may note that the two spellings gern and gerne mean the same and are not inflected in any manner. It is purely a dialectical variation. One may use either of them in their written language.

This particle can be used to know the likes and preferences of the other person. One can ask about food, drink, free time activities and so on even without using the particle but its use adds a touch of like or preference to the sentence. The following table shows some of the commonly used questions and answers with the particle gern. The verbs have been conjugated in the ‚du' form. Similar expressions can be formed in the ‚Sie' form.

	German Sentence	English equivalent
	Was isst du gern?	*What do you like to eat?*
1	Ich esse Fisch sehr gern.	*I like to eat fish.*
	Ich esse Gurke nicht so gern.	*I don't like to eat cucumber.*
	Was trinkst du gern?	*What do you like to drink?*
2	Ich trinke gern Kaffee.	*I like to drink coffee.*
	Ich trinke Wein nicht so gern.	*I don't like to drink wine.*
	Was machst du gern?	*What do you like to do?*
3	Ich schreibe sehr gern.	*I like to write.*
	Ich faulenze nicht so gern.	*I don't like to laze around.*
	Isst du gern Salat?	*Do you like to eat salad?*
4	Ja, sehr gern.	*Yes, very much.*
	Nein, nicht so gern.	*No, not that much.*
	Trinkst du gern Apfelsaft?	*Do you like to drink Apple juice?*
5	Ja, sehr gern.	*Yes, very much.*
	Nein, nicht so gern.	*No, not that much.*

There is thus no fixed position of adding <u>gern</u> to the sentence. One may add it at any location that is found appropriate to the context.

2.3.4 schon

The particle **schon** is used to express a strong opinion or a sense of authority. There is no exact equivalent in English for this particle in English. The following sentences may be consiedred a guideline to understand the different uses of the particle ‚schon'.

	German Sentence	English equivalent
1	Ich hatte dir **schon** gesagt!	*I had **already** told you!*
2	Sie können sich **schon** anmelden.	*You can **very well** register yourself.*
3	Wir sind seit **schon** einer Stunde hier gekommen.	*We have been here **pretty much** since an hour.*

2.3.5 sofort

The particle **sofort** is used to express willingness to do a particular task. It is used similar to the English expressions like 'right away' and 'immediately'. Following sentences provide a basic idea of the same.

		German Sentence	English equivalent
1	Frage	Hast du die Tickets gekauft?	*Have you bought the tickets?*
	Antwort	Nein, ich kaufe sie **sofort**.	*No, I will buy them immediately/right now.*
2	Frage	Haben Sie die E-Mail geschickt?	*Have you sent the email?*
	Antwort	Ja, ich habe sie **sofort** gestern geschickt.	*Yes, I sent it yesterday right away.*

2.4 Indefinite person man/jemand/niemand

There are a number of formal situations wherein the spoken or written language should be as polite as possible. This can be done better with the help of indefinite pronouns. In order to help express information in an indefinite third person, the indefinite pronouns <u>man</u>, <u>jemand</u> and <u>niemand</u> are used. These pronouns are always singular and the corresponding verb conjugations are same as that of the third person singular i.e. er/sie/es.

It may be noted that the pronouns man / jemand / niemand are used for persons only. While referring to things, there are indefinite objects etwas / alles / nichts which have been explained in the next section.

Following table explains this concept with example sentences.

	Meaning	German Sentence	English equivalent
man	*one*	**Man** darf hier nicht rauchen!	*One must not smoke here!*
		Beim Fahren muss **man** immer vorsichtig sein.	*One must always be careful while driving.*
jemand	*someone*	**Jemand** ist mit mir gekommen.	*Someone has come with me.*
		Ich treffe **jemanden**.	*I am meeting **someone**.*
niemand	*nobody*	**Niemand** ist mit mir gekommen.	*Nobody has come with me.*
		Ich treffe **niemanden**.	*I am meeting **nobody**.*

The pronouns jemand and niemand can have endings as per cases but there is no hard and fast rule that the endings have to be added.

2.5 Indefinite object etwas/alles/nichts

In German, just like an indefinite person, there exists an expression for an indefinite object too. These are used in all types of spoken and written instances. These pronouns are also always singular. However, unlike the indefinite person which can be used as the sole pronoun of the sentence, indefinite objects are used more often with other pronouns. Examples are as follows.

	Meaning	German Sentence	English equivalent
etwas	*something*	Gestern hatte ich **etwas** gelesen.	*Yesterday I had read **something**.*
		Möchten Sie **etwas** zu essen oder trinken?	*Would you like **something** to eat or drink?*
alles	*everything*	Heute will ich **alles** lesen.	*I want to read **everything** today.*
		Wie kannst du **alles** essen?	*How can you eat **everything**?*
nichts	*nothing*	Morgen kaufe ich **nichts**.	*I am going to buy **nothing** tomorrow.*
		Warum hast du **nichts** gegessen?	*Why have you eaten **nothing**?*

In the initial stages, the distinction between the words ‚alle' and ‚alles' has to be understood. In any context, ‚alle' refers to 'all' (people or things) whereas ‚alles' refers to 'everything'. Similarly, the distinction between the words ‚nicht' and ‚nichts' has to be understood. In any context, ‚nicht' refers to the negation word used to negate a verb whereas ‚nichts' refers to 'nothing'. With practice, one can easily use the same with distinction and confidence.

2.6 Adverbs to indicate uncertainty – irgendetwas, irgend + …

During conversations, it may happen that certain aspects spoken may be uncertain and details may be awaited. German has the provision to use a number of words with the prefix ‚irgend' to express such uncertainty where certain random information is expressed. Following are some such words with their meanings.

Adverb	Meaning	Adverb	Meaning
irgendwann	*sometime/anytime*	irgendwas	*something/anything*
iregendwohin	*(to) somewhere*	irgendwer	*anyone*
irgendein(e)	*any*	irgendwie	*anyhow/somehow*
irgendetwas	*something*	irgendwo	*anywhere/somewhere*
irgendjemand	*anyone*	irgendwoher	*(from) somewhere*

The following table provides example sentences with English equivalents.

Adverb	Satz	German Sentence	English equivalent
irgendwann	Frage	Wann treffen wir uns?	*When are we meeting?*
	Antwort	Wir können uns **irgendwann** treffen.	*We can meet **anytime**.*
iregendwohin	Frage	Wohin ist er gegangen?	*Where has he gone?*
	Antwort	Er ist **irgendwohin** gegangen.	*He has gone **somewhere**.*
irgendein(e)	Frage	Was möchtest du trinken?	*What would you like to drink?*
	Antwort	**Irgendein** Saft bitte!	***Any** juice please!*
irgendetwas	Frage	Was hat er gestern gesagt?	*What has he said yesterday?*
	Antwort	Er hat einfach **irgendetwas** gesagt.	*He just said **something**.*
irgendjemand	Frage	Wer kann mitkommen?	*Who can come along?*
	Antwort	**Irgendjemand** kann sicherlich mitkommen.	***Anyone** can surely come along.*
irgendwas	Frage	Was brauchst du?	*What do you need?*
	Antwort	Gibt es **irgendwas** zu lesen?	*Is there **something** to read?*
irgendwer	Frage	Wer kann Deutsch sprechen?	*Who can speak German?*
	Antwort	**Irgendwer** kann Deutsch sprechen.	***Anyone** can speak German.*
irgendwie	Frage	Was muss ich tun?	*What should I do?*
	Antwort	Sie müssen alles **irgendwie** schaffen.	*You must **somehow** manage everything.*
irgendwo	Frage	Wo gehen wir am Wochenende?	*Where shall we go for the weekend?*
	Antwort	Wir gehen **irgendwo**.	*We shall go **somewhere**.*
irgendwoher	Frage	Woher ist sie gekommen?	*Where from has she come?*
	Antwort	Sie ist **irgendwoher** gekommen.	*She has come from **somewhere**.*

It can be seen that the English equivalents are same for a few adverbs. Thus it is recommended that no one to one correspondence is established between the two languages.

The expressions mentioned in the table above are from everyday spoken German. These are generally not used in written German because there are certain etiquettes of language that need to be followed while writing since it is an indirect form of communication.

2.7 Interrogative articles Was für ein(e) and Welche

In A1, the Interrogative article <u>welcher</u> was seen in various cases. However, when someone wants to seek information about something new, the interrogative article Was für ein(e) is used. Welcher is equivalent to 'which' whereas Was für ein is equivalent to 'what sort of / what kind of'. It may be noted that 'Was für ein' is a phrase and the preposition für is <u>not followed</u> by the accusative article 'einen'.

Following table shall provide further clarity by comparing the two interrogative articles.

	Was für ein(e) ...?	**Welcher/-e/-es ...?**
	<u>Asking something new</u>	<u>Asking known things</u>
Frage	Was für ein Buch möchtest du lesen?	Welches Buch gehört dir?
	What kind of book would you like to read?	*Which book belongs to you?*
Antwort	Ich möchte Komödie.	Dieses Buch gehört mir.
	I would like comedy.	*This book belongs to me.*

Thus while asking for unknown information one can use 'Was für ein' and to refer to known aspects, one can use the various forms of 'Welche'.

3. Verbs

3.1 Accusative and Dative Verbs in German

The concept of verbs and cases has been introduced to a great extent at A1 level. Cases mostly affect the inflexion of nouns, adjectives and articles. The case itself at times is decided by the verb used in the sentence. There are certain verbs that are always used with either Accusative or Dative cases.

Verbs used with the Accusative case always convey a direct action while those with Dative case convey an action that requires an indirect object. It is advisable that instead of memorizing the lists, one understands the use of these type of verbs with the help of sentences. Some of the examples are as follows (The complete list is pretty long and only a few verbs have been given here)

	Verb	German Sentence	English equivalent
AKKUSATIV	brauchen	Ich brauche einen Stift.	*I need a pen.*
	essen	Isst du keinen Salat?	*Don't you eat salad?*
	fragen	Immer fragt er nur mich.	*He always asks only me.*
	haben	Sie hat eine Orange.	*She has an orange.*
	halten	Ich halte dich.	*I am holding you.*
	kaufen	Wir kaufen ein Auto.	*We are buying a car.*
	kochen	Kocht ihr gern Hühnersuppe?	*Do you like to cook chicken soup?*
	lieben	Ich liebe dich.	*I love you.*
	machen	Sie machen ein Picknick.	*They are doing a picknick.*
	mögen	Mögen Sie mich?	*Do you like me?*
	nehmen	Wir nehmen einen Katalog.	*We are taking a catalogue.*
	sehen	Er sieht einen Film.	*He is seeing a film.*
	trinken	Trinkst du gern Kaffee?	*Do you like to drink cofee?*
DATIV	antworten	Ich antworte dir.	*I am answering you*
	danken	Er dankt ihm.	*He is thanking him.*
	folgen	Wer folgt mir?	*Who is following me?*
	gefallen	Deine Augen gefallen mir.	*I like your eyes.*
	gehören	Wem gehört dieses Buch?	*Whom does this book belong to?*
	gratulieren	Ich gratuliere dir.	*I congratulate you.*
	helfen	Ich helfe dir.	*I am helping you.*
	passen	Dieses Hemd passt Ihnen gut.	*This shirt suits you.*
	passieren	Mir ist viel Gluck passiert.	*I went through a lot of good luck.*
	sagen	Bitte sagen Sie mir.	*Please tell me.*
	schmecken	Wie schmeckt dir den Salat?	*How do you like the salad?*
	sprechen	Sprich mit mir, irgendwas du willst.	*Speak to me anything you want.*

3.2 Reflexive Verbs

In most of the European languages, one can find verbs which indicate a reflexive form. Reflexive form is used when the object of the verb is same as that of the subject. The object may be Akkusativ or Dativ. Reflexive verbs indicate a reflexive action with respect to the subject. Reflexive verbs are written between the pronoun and its reflexive counterpart. Following table provides information on the pronouns for reflexive verbs in the Accusative and Dative cases.

	Reflexivpronomen	
	Akkusativ	**Dativ**
ich	mich	mir
du	dich	dir
er/sie/es	sich	
wir	uns	
ihr	euch	
sie/Sie	sich	

It can be seen that the reflexive pronouns are similar to the personal pronouns in the accusative or dative cases. The only exception is that for the third person (singular and plural) and the formal 'Sie', the reflexive pronoun is **sich**. One can also see that the reflexive pronouns for first and second person singular are distinct for the two cases while they are the same for all the others.

In order to easily remember whether a verb is reflexive or not, one can remember it by writing the pronoun **sich** with the verb and using it accordingly. For reflexive verbs with separable prefix, the same rules as applicable for other verbs with seperable prefix apply. The conjugated part of the verb is written in the second position and the seperable prefix is written at the end of the sentence. If a modal verb is present, the entire verb in its infinitive form is written at the end of the sentence.

The following table provides a number of example sentences. There are some sentences with the accusative case while a few with the dative case. This can be understood by ascertaining whether the object is direct or indirect. Certain examples with modal verbs have also been included to cover major types of sentences. Since the concept of reflexive verbs is used less often in English, the English equivalents have not been given here as they may seem unintelligible.

Reflexive Verb	Example Sentence
sich ansehen	**Wir** sehen **uns** in dem Fenster an.
sich anziehen	**Ich** ziehe **mich** glücklich an.
sich ärgern	Warum ärgerst **du dich**?
sich aufregen	**Ich** rege **mich** über die Prüfung auf.
sich auskennen	Können **wir uns** auskennen?
sich austauschen	Gestern hatten **wir uns** für den Platz ausgetauscht.
sich beeilen	**Du** musst **dich** für den Film beeilen.
sich beschweren	Warum wollen **Sie sich** beschweren?
sich einladen	Herr Bean **lädt** sich immer selbst **ein**.
sich engagieren	**Ich** habe **mich** beim Schreiben engagiert
sich entschuldigen	**Sie** müssen **sich** für die Verspätung entschuldigen.
sich erholen	Hast **du dich** die Geschenke erholt?
sich erlauben	**Ich** kann **mich** beim Rauchen nicht erlauben.
sich erkälten	Seien **Sie sich** vorsichtig, nicht zu erkälten.
sich freuen	**Ich** freue **mich** auf das Konzert.
sich gewöhnen	**Sie** sollen **sich** mit dem Wetter gewöhnen.
sich hinlegen	**Ich** möchte **mich** nach der Arbeit hinlegen.
sich kaufen	**Ich** kaufe **mir** die Gemüse.
sich konzentrieren	Es ist zu laut. **Ich** kann **mich** nicht konzentrieren.
sich kümmern	Im kalten Wetter müssen **Sie sich** kümmern.
sich langweilen	Worauf langweilst **du dich**?
sich qualifizieren	**Ich** habe **mich** für das nächste Sprachniveau qualifiziert.
sich treffen	**Wir** treffen **uns** morgen nach dem Unterricht.
sich umdrehen	Nach der Kirche sollen **Sie sich** umdrehen.
sich umziehen	**Wir** sind **uns** schon einen Monat vor umgezogen.
sich unterhalten	Gestern haben **wir uns** über diesem Thema unterhaltet.
sich verabschieden	Nach dem Essen sind **wir uns** verabschieden.
sich verirren	In der großen Stadt sind **wir uns** zuerst verirren.
sich verletzen	Er hat einen Unfall und **(er)** (hat) **sich** verletzt.
sich vorstellen	Zuerst stelle **ich mich** vor.
sich waschen	Morgens wasche **ich mir** die Augen.

3.3 Modal verbs in Simple Past Tense (Modalverben im Präteritum)

Following table summarizes the modal verbs in simple past tense.

Präsens	dürfen	können	mögen	müssen	sollen	wollen
Präteritum	**durften**	**konnten**	**mochten**	**mussten**	**sollten**	**wollten**
ich	durfte	konnte	mochte	musste	sollte	wollte
du	durftest	konntest	mochtest	musstest	solltest	wolltest
er/sie/es	durfte	konnte	mochte	musste	sollte	wollte
wir	durften	konnten	mochten	mussten	sollten	wollten
ihr	durftet	konntet	mochtet	musstet	solltet	wolltet
sie/Sie	durften	konnten	mochten	mussten	sollten	wollten

In German, modal verbs play a very important role to indicate ability or permission to perform an action or to avoid an action from being performed. Modal verbs in Präteritum do the same to report something in the simple past tense. The verb conjugation pattern is same as other verbs in Präteritum. The first person and third person singular have the same conjugation.

In English such a concept is not present as exclusively as in German. Thus the following table provides the nearest meanings.

Modalverb (Präsens)	Meaning	Modalverb (Präteritum)	Meaning
dürfen	*allow*	durften	*was/were allowed to*
können	*can*	konnten	*could*
mögen	*like*	mochten	*liked*
müssen	*must*	mussten	*had to*
sollen	*should*	sollten	*should have*
wollen	*want*	wollten	*wanted*

The following table provides certain sentences using each of these modal verbs in the simple past tense (Präteritum). English equivalents have been given along but they should not be taken as a direct translation of the expression written in German.

Verb	German Sentence	English equivalent
durften	Ich durfte mittags schlafen.	*I was allowed to sleep at noons.*
konnten	Konntest du am Wochenende Urlaub machen?	*Were you able to go on vacation in the weekend? (Past tense)*
mochten	Mochte er Fisch essen?	*He liked eating fish?*
mussten	Er musste abends englische Bücher lesen.	*He had to read English books in the evenings.*
sollten	Sie sollten mir sagen.	*You should have told me.*
wollten	Wir wollten ihn anrufen.	*We wanted to call him on phone.*

Modal verbs in the simple past tense are used extensively to express how things were at a certain point in time in the past. However, it is important to note that in German, the modal verbs in simple past tense are used only to tell something that actually had happened.

There are times when the speaker wants to express himself/herself in such a manner as to tell how things should have been in the past or make polite requests. This is done using the subjunctive form (Konjunktiv II) of modal verbs which has been discussed in the later chapters in this book.

3.4 The verb 'werden'

The verb **werden** is a versatile verb. It generally translates to 'to become' in English. It is used in almost all the tenses in different ways. In the present tense it can be used to describe the immediate future condition of the subject with respect to education or profession. It can be used to convey the age, one is going to complete on a birthday that is about to come.

In the past tense, the verb **werden** can be used to describe a state that was achieved by the subject at a certain point in time in the past. For the simple future tense, the verb is used in a format similar to the modal verbs. It is explained in brief here and is studied in detail at B1 and higher levels.

Following table summarizes the same with suitable examples.

Tense	Verb form	German Sentence	English equivalent
Präteritum	wurden	Er **wurde** glücklich, nach der Führerscheinprüfung bestehen.	*He became happy after passing the driver's license exam.*
Perfekt	ist geworden	Sie **ist** eine Ingenieurin **geworden**.	*She has become an Engineer.*
Präsens	werden	Sie **wird** Ingenieurin.	*She will become an Engineer.*
		Wir **werden** glücklich.	*We will be happy.*
		Ich **werde** 27 dieses Jahr.	*This year I'm turning 27.*
Futur I	werden + infinitiv	Ich **werde** viele Bücher **lesen**.	*I'm going to read many books.*

The future tense shall be introduced at B1 level along with an elaborate idea of the verb **werden**. The underlined parts in the English equivalents are just the nearest meanings of the conjugations of the verb **werden** in various tenses. These may not be taken as direct translations. The verb werden is also used to express wishes. This has been discussed in the chapter on Konjunktiv II in this book.

4. The Genitive Case (Genitiv)

4.1 About the Case

This is the fourth Case learnt in German. This case is called as **Genitiv** and it indicates the possession of nouns. The Nominative case only describes the subject and helps to make sentences with only the subject and the verb. In the Accusative case, a direct object is introduced to the sentence. Direct object is that which directly receives the action indicated by the verb of the sentence. However, sentences may have additional objects that do not directly receive the action but convey the action. Such objects are indirect objects or Dative objects.

With a keen observation, one can infer that the Genitive case is a way in which, one can indicate the relation between objects. While this case is not used as widely as the other three, it is interesting to learn it as it can reduce the length of sentences by establishing relations between the object(s) and/or subject. Some examples of formation of Genitive are as follows.

Expression	Genitiv
der Arbeitstisch von Gourav	Gouravs Arbeitstisch
die Tasche von Gouri	Gouris Tasche
das Handy von Shreyas	Shreyas' Handy
die Kinder von Kishor	Kishors Kinder

It can be seen that to express the object in Genitive case, an **s** or **es** is added after the subject if it is the name of a person irrespective of the gender (proper noun). For all other nouns that indicate objects, this is done only if the noun is masculine or neuter. The feminine and plural forms of the nouns do not have a **s** or **es** attached to it in the Genitive Case (elaborated in the next section). If the last letter of the noun indicating the subject is s or x or z, only an apostrophe is marked as in Shreyas' or Topaz'. It can also be seen that instead of using the preposition 'von', one can express the idea with the help of the Genitive case in a concise manner.

The general question in Genitive Case would start with the Interrogative pronoun **Wessen** which is used to ask the relation of the object with a person. This word generally corresponds to 'whose' in English which asks possession of an object. Examples considering the expressions mentioned in the table above are as follows.

Frage	Antwort
Wessen Arbeitstisch ist das?	Das ist Gouravs Arbeitstisch.
Wessen Tasche ist das?	Das ist Gouris Tasche.
Wessen Handy ist das?	Das ist Shreyas' Handy.
Wessen Kinder sind das?	Das sind Kishors Kinder.

4.2 Sentence Structure

The sentence structure for the Genitive case is a continuation of the ones learnt earlier. The subject is generally written in the first position followed by the conjugated or auxiliary or modal verb in the second position. The indirect object (Dative object) along with the article is written after the conjugated verb. The direct object (Accusative object) along with the article is written after the Dative object. The Genitive object is written towards the end of the sentence right before the end element (Partizip II or separated verb prefix etc). More examples on this have been given towards the end of this chapter.

4.3 Articles used and inflexion

Following table provides information on various articles used in the Genitive Case along with example sentences and meanings. Please note that the meanings are indicative and should not be taken as a one to one correspondence or translation. It may also be noted that for masculine and neutral common nouns, if the last letter is s/x/z the ending is s or es and the apostrophe is not added. i.e for <u>Kurs</u> one writes <u>Kurses</u> and not <u>Kurs'</u>

	Article	German sentence	English equivalent
Indefinite Articles (Unbestimmterartikeln)			
Masculine	eines	Ich lese ein Buch **eines** Mannes.	*I read a man's book.*
Feminine	einer	Ich lese ein Buch **einer** Frau.	*I read a lady's book.*
Neutral	eines	Ich repariere ein Spielzeug **eines** Kindes.	*I repair a child's toy.*
Plural	-	*Meaningful sentence cannot be generally formed in plural*	
Definite Articles (Bestimmterartikeln)			
Masculine	des	Ich lese ein Buch **des** Mannes.	*I read the man's book.*
Feminine	der	Ich lese ein Buch **der** Frau.	*I read the lady's book.*
Neutral	des	Ich repariere ein Spielzeug **des** Kindes.	*I repair the child's toy.*
Plural	der	Ich schreibe die Namen **der** Leute.	*I write people's names.*
Negation Articles (Negationartikeln)			
Masculine	keines	Er folgt Anleitungen **keines** Mannes.	*He follows no man's instructions.*
Feminine	keine	Sie folgt Anleitungen **keiner** Frau.	*She follows no woman's instructions.*
Neutral	keines	Ich will Spielzeuge **keines** Kindes reparieren.	*I don't want to repair any child's toys.*
Plural	keiner	Hier gibt es Schuhe **keiner** Leute.	*There aren't any people's shoes here.*

Following table summarizes possessive article forms used with the Genitive case.

Pronomen	maskulin	feminin	neutrum	plural
ich	meines	meiner	meines	meiner
du	deines	deiner	deines	deiner
er	seines	seiner	seines	seiner
sie	ihres	ihrer	ihres	ihrer
es	seines	seiner	seines	seiner
wir	unseres	unserer	unseres	unserer
ihr	eures	eurer / euerer	eures	eurer / euerer
sie	ihres	ihrer	ihres	ihrer
Sie	Ihres	Ihrer	Ihres	Ihrer

Following are certain examples of the use of these possessive articles in Genitive case for all the pronouns.

	German Sentence	English equivalent
ich	Bist du die Freundin **meines** Sohns?	*Are you **my** son's friend?*
du	Ich bin der Freund **deiner** Schwester.	*I am **your** sister's friend.*
er	Er ist ein Student **seiner** Uni.	*He is a student of **his** University.*
sie	Sie gab ihm die Nummer **ihres** Handys.	*She gave him **her** cell number.*
es	Das ist ein Kind **seiner** Eltern.	*This is a child of **its** parents.*
wir	Wir haben das Ergebnis **unserer** Prüfung bekommen.	*We have got the result of **our** Exam.*
ihr	Habt ihr die Seiten **eures** Buchs gelesen?	*Have you read the pages of **your** book?*
sie	Sie haben die Äpfel **ihres** Baums gegessen.	*They have eaten the apples of **their** tree.*
Sie	Haben Sie das Haus **Ihres** Freundes verkauft?	*Have you sold **your** friend's house?*

Although it is very rare that one makes a sentence with all the three cases in it, one can know the use of this case to improve the power of expression. Following sentences try to demonstrate a way in which a sentence in the Perfekt tense with all the three cases and genders can be made.

Example 1: All masculine singular nouns

Ich habe meinem Freund einen Hund meines Bruders gegeben.

Pos	1	2	3	4	5	6
Element	Ich	habe	meinem Freund	einen Hund	meines Bruders	gegeben.
	Subjekt	Verb	Dativ	Akkusativ	Genitiv	Satzende

Since all the nouns are masculine, the articles **meinem**, **einen** and **meines** have been used to indicate the Dative, Accusative and Genitive cases respectively. Since a masculine noun <u>Bruder</u> is used in the Genitive case, the suffix **s** is added to it to make it <u>Bruders</u>.

Example 2: All feminine singular nouns

Ich habe meiner Freundin eine Katze meiner Schwester gegeben.

Pos	1	2	3	4	5	6
Element	Ich	habe	meiner Freundin	eine Katze	meiner Schwester	gegeben.
	Subjekt	Verb	Dativ	Akkusativ	Genitiv	Satzende

Since all the nouns are feminine, the articles **meiner**, **eine** and **meiner** have been used to indicate the Dative, Accusative and Genitive cases respectively. Since a feminine noun Schwester is used in the Genitive case, no suffix is added to it.

Example 3: All neutral singular nouns

Ich habe meinem Mädchen ein Handy meines Kindes gegeben.

Pos	1	2	3	4	5	6
Element	Ich	habe	meinem Mädchen	ein Handy	meines Kindes	gegeben.
	Subjekt	Verb	Dativ	Akkusativ	Genitiv	Satzende

Since all the nouns are neutral, the articles **meinem**, **ein** and **meines** have been used to indicate the Dative, Accusative and Genitive cases respectively. Since a neutral noun Kind is used in the Genitive case, the suffix **es** is added to it to make it Kindes.

Example 4: All plural nouns

Ich habe meinen Kindern Spielzeuge meiner Brüder gegeben.

Pos	1	2	3	4	5	6
Element	Ich	habe	meinen Kindern	Spielzeuge	meiner Brüder	gegeben.
	Subjekt	Verb	Dativ	Akkusativ	Genitiv	Satzende

Since all the nouns are plural, the articles **meinen** and **meiner** have been used to indicate the Dative and Genitive cases respectively. Since there is no plural form of indefinite articles, the Accusative object is written all by itself in the plural form. Since a plural form of the noun Bruder is used in the Genitive case, no suffix is added to it and the plural form Brüder is written as it is.

Thus with the use of all the cases, one can easily understand the doer of the action, the receiver of the action, the indirect beneficiary of the action and the owner of the direct object. This sums up all the German Cases i.e Nominativ, Akkusativ, Dativ and Genitiv.

5. Prepositions for A2 (Präpositionen)

Prepositions have been introduced to a great extent at the A1 level for better acquaintance. Three groups of prepositions have been learnt so far. One of the groups comprises of prepositions that are always used with the accusative case while another has prepositions that are always used with the dative case. There is a third group of prepositions that can be used with either the accusative or dative case. This depends on whether the verb used in the sentence indicates any kind of movement or not. This has been given in detail in the book titled 'Let's Learn German A1' by the author of this book.

At A2 level, some more prepositions have been added to the list. A consolidated table is as follows.

Gruppe 1 **Präposition + Akkusativ** **Wohin?**		Gruppe 2 **Präposition + Akkusativ** **oder** **Präposition + Dativ**		Gruppe 3 **Präposition + Dativ** **Wo?**	
durch	*through*	in	*in*	zu	*to*
für	*for*	an	*at/on (wall)*	von	*of/from*
gegen	*against*	neben	*next to*	nach	*after/to*
ohne	*without*	auf	*on (table)*	mit	*with*
um	*around*	zwischen	*between*	aus	*from/out of*
bis	*until*	vor	*in front*	bei	*at*
entlang	*along*	hinter	*behind*	seit	*since*
wider	*contrary to*	unter	*under*	gegenüber	*opposite to*
		über	*above*	außer	*except*

In Gruppe 2 i.e. Wechselpräpositionen, one can determine the case (Akkusativ oder Dativ) by looking at the verbs and their action in the sentence. If the verb indicates a movement (giving rise to the question **Wohin?**), the case shall be Akkusativ while if no movement is indicated (giving rise to the question **Wo?**), the case shall be Dativ. Some of the prominent verbs to make out this difference are as follows although they seem similar and convey similar meanings.

Wohin? **(Akkusativ)**	setzen	stellen	legen	hängen
Wo? (Dativ)	sitzen	stehen	liegen	hängen

Following sentences try to bring out this difference.

Akkusativ (Wohin?)	Dativ (Wo?)
Ich setze die Lampe <u>neben</u> **den** Stuhl.	Die Lampe sitzt <u>neben</u> **dem** Stuhl.
Er stellt die Flasche <u>auf</u> **den** Tisch.	Die Flasche steht <u>auf</u> **dem** Tisch.
Sie legt das Handy <u>unter</u> **die** Bücher.	Das Handy liegt <u>unter</u> **den** Büchern.
Ich hänge das Bild <u>an</u> **die** Tür.	Das Bild hängt <u>an</u> **der** Tür.

There are some verbs that are generally used with certain fixed prepositions and cases. Following examples demonstrate the same. The list is however not limited to these.

	Verb	Preposition	Example
Akkusativ	denken	an	Ich denke an das Konzert.
	warten	auf	Er wartet auf den Zug.
	sich ärgern	über	Sie ärgert sich über den schlechten Salat.
	sich erinnern	an	Wir erinnern uns an die Schulzeit.
	sich freuen	auf	Ich freue mich auf die Prüfung.
	sich freuen	über	Freuen Sie sich über das Ergebnis?
	sich interessieren	für	Sie interessiert sich für den Sprachkurs.
	sich kümmern	um	Er kümmert sich um die Gesundheit.
Dativ	arbeiten	bei	Ich arbeite bei einer Firma.
	kommen	aus	Er kommt aus Indien.
	sprechen	mit	Wer hat mit wem gesprochen?
	studieren	an	Ich studiere an dem Institut.
	sich verabreden	mit	Wir verabreden uns mit ihnen.

While learning German prepositions one may frequently come across an example to indicate the difference between the use of accusative and dative case for the same preposition. This example is generally taught by a number of German teachers and hence couldn't be omitted here. [2]

warten auf + Akkusativ z.B: Ich warte auf **den** Bus.	There is a movement in time *I wait for the Bus.*
warten auf + Dativ z.B: Ich warte auf **dem** Bus.	There is no movement at all *I wait (sit) on the Bus.*

Another widely given example is of the reflexive verb **sich freuen** which may be used as follows [2]

sich freuen **auf** etwas (Akkusativ) : Happy about something about to happen

sich freuen **über** etwas (Akkusativ) : Happy about something that has happened

5.1 New Prepositions with Accusative and Dative cases for A2

Prepositions can be used to indicate movement, location and so on. Some prepositions are always used with Akkusativ while some are always used with Dativ. Four additional prepositions to be learnt at A2 level are as follows.

Case	Preposition	Meaning	Example Sentence
Akkusativ	entlang	*along*	Ich laufe entlang den Garten.
	wider	*contrary to*	Willst du etwas wider meine Meinung sagen?
Dativ	gegenüber	*opposite to*	Die Tür steht gegenüber der Wand.
	außer	*except*	Niemand außer ihm hat der Hausaufgabe gemacht.

5.2 Prepositions with Genitive Case

Just like there are a certain prepositions used exclusively with the Accusative or Dative cases, there are a few used exclusively with the Genitive case as well. Since the Genitive case indicates the genesis of the direct object, these prepositions are used to refer to a certain noun accordingly. Following table tries to put together Genitive prepositions with examples. English translations have been avoided to enable the reader build competence of understanding the sentences in German itself.

Preposition	Meaning	Example Sentence
wegen	*because of*	Wegen meiner Eltern Unterstützung habe ich Deutsch gelernt.
während	*during*	Es war interessante, während des Kurses Deutsch lernen.
trotz	*in spite of*	Trotz der schlechten Vorbereitung hat er die Prüfung bestanden.
innerhalb	*inside of*	Es gibt so viel zu essen innerhalb des Hauses.
außerhalb	*outside of*	Es gibt so viel zu tun außerhalb des Hauses.

5.3 Question words with prepositions

Prepositions are excellent fillers used in speech to specify the state of various nouns, be it with respect to position or time. As the language learning is advanced, one can learn to use prepositions along with the W-Fragen to ask questions. This section shall focus on the combined use of words used to form W-Fragen and various suitable prepositions.

In German, due to the presence of the concept of cases and gender distinction, one can find a variety of ways in which this exercise can be done depending on whether the questions have been formulated to ask about persons or about things. The tables in this section indicate the way in which questions are formed and the way in which various question words can be formulated or inflected and used to ask about persons and things accordingly.

A basic table with questions without the use of prepositions is as follows.

Fall	Frage	Antwort	Bedeutung
Nominativ	**Wer** schreibt?	Gourav schreibt.	Wer – Person
	Was schreibt?	Der Stift schreibt.	Was – Sache
Akkusativ	**Wen** zeichnest du?	Ich zeichne einen Mann.	Wen – Person
	Was zeichnest du?	Ich zeichne einen Stift.	Was – Sache
Dativ	**Wem** passt die Hose?	Die Hose passt seiner Freundin.	Wem – Person
	Was passt seiner Freundin?	Die Hose passt seiner Freundin.	Was – Sache

The above table has been formed without using any prepositions with the questions. But in day to day spoken German, it is a rare occurrence that questions are asked without prepositions. Using prepositions, one can ask questions for a person or a thing. There is a more or less fixed pattern followed while forming the question phrases which is as follows.

While <u>asking</u> for a <u>person</u>:
   Präposition + Wen (Akkusativ) / Präposition + Wem (Dativ) z.B: für wen? / mit wem?

It may be noted that the Nominativ case cannot be used to ask questions with prepositions. This is because questions with prepositions are addressed to a person which automatically makes the question phrase to take the accusative or dative case according to the flow of action in the sentence according to the verb.

Similarly, while <u>asking</u> for a <u>thing</u>:
   Wo + Präposition / Wo + r + Präposition (first letter vowel) z.B: Wofür / Woran

It can be seen that when asking for a person, the preposition is written before the question word and the two aren't combined to form a single word whereas while asking for a thing the question word 'Wo' and the preposition are combined and written as a single word. If the first letter of the preposition is a vowel, in order to ease pronunciation, the letter 'r' is added in between.

While <u>answering</u> a question asked for a <u>person</u>, the following response is generally used:
   Ja, Präposition + Pronomen (Akkusativ / Dativ). z.B: Ja, für ihn/Ja, mit ihm.

While <u>answering</u> a question asked for a <u>thing</u>, the following response is generally used:
   Ja, da + Präposition / Ja, da + r + Präposition (first letter vowel). z.B dafür, daran

A summary of this concept and examples with questions and answers has been given in the following tables.

<u>While asking and responding a question for a person:</u>

		Akkusativ	**Dativ**
Question	Format	Präposition + Wen	Präposition + Wem
	Example	für wen?	mit wem?
Answer (Positive)	Format	Präposition + Pronomen (Akkusativ / Dativ)	
	Example	Ja, für ihn	Ja, mit ihm
Answer (Negation)	Format	nicht Präposition + Pronomen (Akkusativ / Dativ)	
	Example	Nein, nicht für ihn.	Nein, nicht mit ihm.

<u>While asking and responding a question for a thing:</u>

		Preposition starting with consonant	**Preposition starting with vowel (a/e/i/o/u)**
Question	Format	Wo + Präposition	Wo + r + Präposition
	Example	Wofür	Woran
Answer (Positive)	Format	Ja, da + Präposition	Ja, da + r + Präposition
	Example	Ja, dafür.	Ja, daran.
Answer (Negation)	Format	Nein, nicht da + Präposition	Nein, nicht da + r + Präposition
	Example	Nein, nicht dafür.	Nein, nicht daran.

Following three tables summarize the question words and short responses for all the prepositions. For those fields marked with a hyphen (-), question phrases using this pattern cannot be formed as they do not convey meaningful information. Other W-Fragen like 'Wann' may be used with these prepositions.

Akkusativ Präpositionen:

Präposition	**für Personen**		**für Sachen**	
	Frage	**Antwort**	**Frage**	**Antwort**
durch	-	-	Wodurch?	dadurch
für	für wen?	für ihn	Wofür?	dafür
gegen	-	-	Wogegen?	dagegen
ohne	ohne wen?	ohne ihn	-	-
um	-	-	Worum?	darum
bis	-	-	-	-
entlang	-	-	-	-
wider	-	-	-	-

It may ne noted that the pronoun 'ihn' shall be replaced with other accusative pronouns according to the subject.

Dativ Präpositionen:

Präposition	für Personen		für Sachen	
	Frage	Antwort	Frage	Antwort
zu	zu wem?	zu ihm	Wozu?	dazu
von	von wem?	von ihm	Wovon?	davon
nach	nach wem?	nach ihm	Wonach?	danach
mit	mit wem?	mit ihm	Womit?	damit
aus	-	-	Woraus?	daraus
bei	bei wem?	bei ihm	Wobei?	dabei
seit	-	-	-	-
gegenüber	gegenüber wem?	gegenüber ihm	-	-
außer	außer wem?	außer ihm	-	-

It may ne noted that the pronoun 'ihm' shall be replaced with other dative pronouns according to the subject.

Wechselpräpositionen:

Präposition	für Personen		für Sachen	
	Frage (Akk)	Frage (Dat)	Frage	Antwort
in	-	-	Worin?	darin
an	-	-	Woran?	daran
neben	-	neben wem?	Woneben?	daneben
auf	auf wen?	-	Worauf?	darauf
zwischen	-	zwischen wem?	Wozwischen?	dazwischen
vor	vor wen?	vor wem?	Wovor?	davor
hinter	-	hinter wem?	Wohinter?	dahinter
unter	-	unter wem?	Worunter?	darunter
über	über wen?	-	Worüber?	darüber

The questions for persons are answered with the personal pronouns in the respective cases along with the preposition.

With this background, one can form sentences using prepositions. In the following tables a variety of sentences with questions and responses have been provided.

Akkusativ Präpositionen:

It may be noted that in the first row, two different ways of answering the question have been given. However as a good practice, one should generally use pronouns in the respective case to answer the questions which can be seen in remaining part of the table and the other succeeding tables as well.

für Personen			
Präposition	**Frage**	**Antwort (Positiv)**	**Antwort (Negation)**
für	Für wen ist der Fisch? Für den Hund?	Ja, für ihn. Ja, der Fisch ist für den Hund.	Nein, nicht für ihn. Nein, der Fisch ist nicht für den Hund.
ohne	Ohne wen machen wir Urlaub? Ohne deinen Bruder?	Ja, leider ohne ihn.	Nein, nicht ohne ihn. Wir machen den Urlaub ohne meine Schwester.
für Sachen			
Präposition	**Frage**	**Antwort (Positiv)**	**Antwort (Negation)**
durch	Wodurch läufst du? Durch den Park?	Ja, dadurch. Ja, ich laufe dadurch.	Nein, nicht dadurch. Ich laufe durch den Garten.
für	Wofür lernst du? Für die Prüfung?	Ja, dafür.	Nein, nicht dafür.
gegen	Wogegen stellst du dich? Gegen den Bahnhof?	Ja, dagegen.	Nein, nicht dagegen.
um	Worum sprichst du? Um die Natur?	Ja, darum.	Nein, nicht darum.

Thus while answering the question with negation; one may do it in three different ways explained in the table as follows.

Frage	Für wen ist dieses Hähnchen? Für den Hund?	
Antwort 1	Nein, nicht für ihn.	*Answer has been given by using the accusative pronoun* **ihn**
Antwort 2	Nein, der Fisch ist nicht für den Hund.	*Answer has been given without the use of pronoun*
Antwort 3	Nein, der Fisch ist für die Katze.	*Answer has been given indicating the actual object (Katze) instead of that mentioned in the question (Hund)*

Dativ Präpositionen:

für Personen			
Präposition	**Frage**	**Antwort (Positiv)**	**Antwort (Negation)**
zu	Zu wem gehst du einfach? Zu deinem Bruder?	Ja, zu ihm.	Nein, nicht zu ihm.
von	Von wem ist dieses Buch? Von deiner Schwester?	Ja, von ihr.	Nein, nicht von ihr.
nach	Nach wem kann ich draußen gehen? Nach unserer Lehrerin?	Ja, nach ihr.	Nein, nicht nach ihr.
mit	Mit wem sprichst du lieber? Mit deiner Freundin?	Ja, lieber immer mit ihr.	Nein, nicht ihr. Mit meinen Eltern spreche ich lieber.
bei	Bei wem bleibst du? Bei Herr Kulkarni?	Ja, bei ihm.	Nein, nicht bei ihm.
außer	Außer wem kannst du nicht lernen? Außer deinen Freunden?	Ja, außer ihnen.	Nein, nicht außer ihnen.

für Sachen			
Präposition	**Frage**	**Antwort (Positiv)**	**Antwort (Negation)**
zu	Wozu antwortest du? Zu den Fragen?	Ja, dazu.	Nein, nicht dazu.
von	Wovon ist die Information? Von dem Sprachkurs?	Ja, davon.	Nein, nicht davon.
nach	Wonach kommt der Bahnhof? Nach der Kirche?	Ja, danach.	Nein, nicht danach.
mit	Womit isst du? Mit dem Löffel?	Ja, damit.	Nein, nicht damit.
aus	Woraus bist du gekommen? Aus deinem Hause?	Ja, daraus.	Nein, nicht daraus.
bei	Wobei arbeitest du? Bei einem Hotel?	Ja, dabei.	Nein, nicht dabei.

Wechselpräpositionen:

für Personen (Akkusativ)			
Präposition	**Frage**	**Antwort (Positiv)**	**Antwort (Negation)**
auf	Auf wen wartest du? Auf deinen Freund?	Ja, auf ihn.	Nein, nicht auf ihn.
vor	Vor wen stellst du den Koffer? Vor die Frau?	Ja, vor sie.	Nein, nicht vor sie.
über	Über wen stellst du das Tuch? Über die Kinder?	Ja, über sie, weil es zu kalt ist.	Nein, nicht über sie.
für Personen (Dativ)			
neben	Neben wem wartest du? Neben dem Mann?	Ja, neben ihm.	Nein, nicht neben ihm.
zwischen	Zwischen wem steht das Kind? Zwischen seinen Eltern?	Ja, zwischen ihnen.	Nein, nicht zwischen ihnen.
vor	Vor wem spricht der Lehrer? Vor den Studenten?	Ja, vor ihnen.	Nein, nicht vor ihnen. Er macht ein Video.
hinter	Hinter wem steht den Koffer? Hinter der Frau?	Ja, hinter ihr.	Nein, nicht hinter ihr.
unter	Unter wem liegt den Teppich? Unter die tanzenden Leute?	Ja, unter ihnen.	Nein, nicht unter ihnen.
für Sachen (Akkusativ und Dativ)			
Präposition	**Frage**	**Antwort (Positiv)**	**Antwort (Negation)**
in	Worin stellst du den Salat? In den Kühlschrank?	Ja, darin.	Nein, nicht darin.
an	Woran hängst du die Tafel? An die Wand?	Ja, daran.	Nein, nicht daran.
neben	Woneben liegt das Buch? Neben dem Stift?	Ja, daneben.	Nein, nicht daneben.
auf	Worauf steht der Laptop? Auf dem Arbeitstisch?	Ja, darauf.	Nein, nicht darauf.
zwischen	Wozwischen steht dein Auto? Zwischen den Häusern?	Ja, dazwischen.	Nein, nicht dazwischen.
vor	Wovor steht er? Vor dem Rathaus?	Ja, davor.	Nein, nicht davor.
hinter	Wohinter fährt das Taxi? Hinter den Berg?	Ja, dahinter.	Nein, nicht dahinter.
unter	Worunter sind die Bücher? Unter dem Koffer?	Ja, darunter.	Nein, nicht darunter.
über	Worüber setzt der Affe? Über dem Baum?	Ja, darüber.	Nein, nicht darüber.

Till this point, questions and answers using prepositions have been demonstrated. However, in German or in any other language, there are a certain verbs and prepositions that go hand in hand. The concept of using question words with prepositions and answers has been elaborated in the following table for such verbs that are always used with fixed prepositions. It may be noted that the examples given in the table are for basic understanding only and the list is not limited to the same as there are many more such verb and preposition pairs to be learnt at higher levels.

	Verb	Preposition	Frage	Antwort
Akkusativ	denken	an	Woran denkst du?	Ich denke an das Konzert.
	warten	auf	Worauf wartet er?	Er wartet auf den Zug.
	sich ärgern	über	Worüber ärgert sie sich?	Sie ärgert sich über den schlechten Salat.
	sich erinnern	an	Woran erinnern sie sich?	Wir erinnern uns an die Schulzeit.
	sich freuen	auf	Worauf freust du dich?	Ich freue mich auf die Prüfung.
	sich freuen	über	Worüber freust du dich?	Ich freue mich über das Prüfungsergebnis.
	sich interessieren	für	Wofür interessiert sie sich?	Sie interessiert sich für den Sprachkurs.
	sich kümmern	um	Worum kümmert er sich?	Er kümmert sich um die Gesundheit.
Dativ	arbeiten	bei	Bei wem arbeiten Sie?	Ich arbeite bei ABC.
	kommen	aus	Woraus kommt er?	Er kommt aus seinem Hause.
	sprechen	mit	Womit sprechen sie täglich?	Ich spreche lieber mit meinen Eltern und Freunden.
	studieren	an	Woran studierst du?	Ich studiere Deutsch an dem Institut.
	sich verabreden	mit	Mit wem verabreden Sie sich?	Wir verabreden uns mit ihnen.

6. Sentence Structure

After having learnt all the cases in German viz. Nominativ, Akkusativ, Dativ and Genitiv, there is a certain revision required, when it comes to formation of sentences at A2 and further levels. This is because with progression in the language, one starts using pronouns instead of nouns in the sentences. There is a specific position for every such sentence element which shall be studied in this chapter. It may also be noted at this point that in German sentences, the most important piece of information is mentioned at the end of the sentence i.e. the last position.

6.1 Sentence with Nominative Case only

In a general sense, a sentence in the Nominativ case comprises of only the subject and the verb followed by an adjective or an adverb or a phrase providing certain further information. Sentences in the Nominative case thus have no object(s).

The general sentence structure is as follows:

	Sentence	Pos 1 Subject	Pos 2 Verb	Pos 3 Satzende
1	Ich komme aus Indien.	Ich	komme	aus Indien.
2	Mein Name ist Gourav.	Mein Name	ist	Gourav.
3	Meine Muttersprache ist Marathi.	Meine Muttersprache	ist	Marathi.

In the second and third sentences the verb is **sein**. It may be noted that whenever this verb is used in the Nominativ, the information on both sides of it is the Subject itself. This means that one says, "Das ist <u>mein</u> Stift" and **not** "~~Das ist meinen Stift~~". The article is not inflected to the Accusative case.

6.2 Sentence with Accusative Case only

The Akkusativ case comes into picture when there is a direct object in the sentence. In addition to this, there are certain accusative prepositions like für, ohne and so on or verbs like haben, kaufen and so on that always take the accusative case which has been explained in this book in the chapter on verbs. Thus a sentence in the Akkusativ case has a subject, conjugated verb, **direct** object and certain further information as the case may be.

The general sentence structure is as follows:

	Sentence	Pos 1 Subject	Pos 2 Verb	Pos 3 Akkusativ objekt	Pos 4 Satzende
1	Ich kaufe einen Apfel. Ich finde ihn frisch.	Ich	kaufe	**einen** Apfel.	-
		Ich	finde	**ihn**	frisch.
2	Ich möchte einen Salat machen.	Ich	möchte	**einen** Salat	machen.
3	Er hatte für den Hund ein Spielzeug gebracht.	Er	hatte	für **den** Hund ein Spielzeug	gebracht.
4	Dieses Buch ist für dich	Dieses Buch	ist	für **dich**.	-

In the above table, a variety of sentences in the accusative case have been given. It can be seen that when the sentence comprises of only the accusative object, the same is written at the sentence end. Accusative pronouns are followed by adjectives or adverbs (Sentence 1). When there are modal verbs or a sentence in Perfekt, the infinitiv or Partizip II is written at the sentence end. It is preceeded by the accusative object (Sentences 2, 3). Sentence 4 demonstrates the use of accusative pronouns.

6.3 Sentence with Dative Case (with or without Accusative object)

The Dativ case comes into picture when there is an indirect object in the sentence. Indirect object is something that conveys the action to the direct object. In addition to this, there are certain dative prepositions like mit, von and so on or verbs like danken, gratulieren and so on that always take the dative case which has been explained in this book in the chapter on verbs. Thus a sentence in the Dativ case has a subject, conjugated verb, **indirect** object and certain further information as the case may be. These sentences may or may not have a direct object if dative prepositions are used.

The general sentence structure is as follows:

	Sentence	Pos 1 Subject	Pos 2 Verb	Pos 3 Dativ objekt	Pos 4 Akkusativ objekt	Pos 4 Satzende
1	Ich spreche mit ihm.	Ich	spreche	mit ihm.	-	-
2	Ich kaufte in dem Markt einen Apfel.	Ich	kaufte	in dem Markt	einen Apfel.	-
3	Ich gebe meinem Freund ein Buch.	Ich	gebe	meinem Freund	ein Buch.	-
4	Er will in der Bäckerei ein Brot kaufen.	Er	will	in der Bäckerei	ein Brot	kaufen.
5	Sie hat in dem Sprachkurs eine Sprache gelernt.	Sie	hat	in dem Sprachkurs	eine Sprache	gelernt.

In the table, a variety of sentences in the dative case have been given. It can be seen that when the sentence comprises of only the dative object, the same is written at the end with the preposition which can make it dative (Sentence 1). The Dative object preceeds the accusative objects if both are written as nouns with or without articles (Sentences 2, 3). When there are modal verbs or a sentence in Perfekt, the infinitiv or Partizip II is written at the sentence end (Sentences 4, 5)

The sentence structure for Genitive case has been discussed at length in the chapter on Genitive Case. Hence a repetition has been avoided here. The reader may carry out a revision of the same before proceeding further.

6.4 Sentences with Pronouns

When the sentence contains both dative and accusative objects, there are four ways of writing the sentence as follows:

1. Both dative and accusative objects written as nouns
2. Dative object written as pronoun and accusative object written as noun
3. Accusative object written as pronoun and dative object written as noun
4. Both dative and accusative object written as pronouns

The sentence structure for these four ways has been demonstrated with examples as follows. It may be noted that pronouns can be used in sentences only when the preceeding sentences have introduced the noun. Following sentences have been written directly with pronouns wherever required for ease of understanding by comparison.

Consider the following sentence:

<u>Er gibt seinem Freund einen Hund</u>.

Er	gibt	seinem Freund	einen Hund.
Nominativ	*Verb*	*Dativ*	*Akkusativ*

This sentence shall be taken up as a reference to explain the four ways as follows:

Dat obj	Akk obj	Sentence	Remarks
noun	noun	Er gibt <u>seinem Freund</u> **einen Hund**.	*Dative noun preceeds* **Accusative noun**
pronoun	noun	Er gibt <u>ihm</u> einen Hund.	*Dative pronoun preceeds Accusative noun*
noun	pronoun	Er gibt **ihn** seinem Freund.	**Accusative pronoun** *preceeds Dative noun*
pronoun	pronoun	Er gibt **ihn** <u>ihm</u>.	**Accusative pronoun** *preceeds Dative pronoun*

It is important to note the positioning of the nouns and pronouns according to their cases in the sentences as demonstrated above. Masculine nouns have been taken as example as the difference in accusative and dative cases can be easily made out.

7. Inflexion of Adjectives (Adjektivdeklination)

7.1 Concept of inflexion

This is an interesting concept learnt at A2 and B1 levels. Although most consider this to be a concept of B1 level, it is recommended that one learns the basics and starts using it at the A2 level itself so that sufficient command can be established while using it at ease for the further levels. This concept gets easier with practice and systematic learning.

Adjectives are the words used to describe nouns. The gender and number of the noun can be understood by looking at the article attached to it. In German, as the <u>case</u> (Nominativ/Akkusativ/Dativ/Genitiv), <u>gender</u> (maskulin/feminin/neutrum) and <u>number</u> (singular/plural) of the noun changes, there are certain changes in the endings of the adjectives as well. This change is called inflexion in English and **Adjektivdeklination** in German. This concept is not observed in English but can be greatly observed in most of the Indian and European languages.

Observe the following statements in English:

1. I have purchased a <u>red</u> apple.　　　2. The <u>red</u> apple was costly.

3. I paid with the <u>blue</u> Credit Card.　　　4. <u>Red</u> apples are cheaper than <u>green</u> apples.

In all the above examples, the adjective <u>red/blue/green</u> remains as it is and there is no inflexion of the same. Also in the last example with plural, there is no inflexion of the adjectives but the noun is inflected from 'apple' to 'apples' as the number changes from singular to plural. Thus generally in English, with change of case or number the noun is inflected and the articles and adjectives are not inflected.

Now observe the following table indicating the same sentences written with German equivalents.

English Sentence	German Equivalent
I have purchased **a** <u>red</u> apple.	Ich habe **einen** <u>roten</u> Apfel gekauft.
The <u>red</u> apple was costly.	**Der** <u>rote</u> Apfel war teuer.
I paid with **the** <u>blue</u> Credit Card.	Ich bezahlte mit **der** <u>blauen</u> Kreditkarte.
<u>Red</u> apples are cheaper than <u>green</u> apples.	<u>Rote</u> Äpfel sind billiger als <u>grüne</u> Äpfel.

It can be seen from the table that as the type of article (indefinite/definite/no article as in statements 1, 2 and 4 respectively) or the case (Dativ in statement 3) and so on changes, the articles and adjectives undergo an inflexion according to the case, number and gender of the noun. This is called Adjektivdeklination in German and is used extensively in German sentences. Following sections shall elaborate this concept with examples.

7.2 Adjektivdeklination for nouns without articles

Following table shows endings that need to be added to the adjectives when no article is used.

	maskulin	feminin	neutrum	Plural
Nominativ	er	e	es	e
Akkusativ	en	e	es	e
Dativ	em	er	em	en
Genitiv	**en**	er	**en**	er

The endings as shown in the table above need to be added to the adjectives according to the gender, number and case of noun in the sentence. Examples are as follows.

maskulin

Case	ending	Example Sentence	Adjektivdeklination
Nominativ	er	Das ist **schneller** Zug.	schnell**er** Zug
Akkusativ	en	Ich sehe **schnellen** Zug.	schnell**en** Zug
Dativ	em	Ich möchte mit **schnellem** Zug reisen.	schnell**em** Zug
Genitiv	**en**	Wie ist der Weg **schnellen** Zuges?	schnell**en** Zuges

feminin

Case	ending	Example Sentence	Adjektivdeklination
Nominativ	e	Das ist **helle** Lampe.	hell**e** Lampe
Akkusativ	e	Ich kaufe **helle** Lampe.	hell**e** Lampe
Dativ	er	Mit **heller** Lampe kann ich lesen.	hell**er** Lampe
Genitiv	er	Was ist die Farbe **heller** Lampe?	hell**er** Lampe

neutrum

Case	ending	Example Sentence	Adjektivdeklination
Nominativ	es	Das ist **ruhiges** Hotel.	ruhig**es** Hotel
Akkusativ	es	Ich suche **ruhiges** Hotel.	ruhig**es** Hotel
Dativ	em	In **ruhigem** Hotel will ich bleiben.	ruhig**em** Hotel
Genitiv	**en**	Wie ist der Name **ruhigen** Hotels?	ruhig**en** Hotels

Plural

Case	ending	Example Sentence	Adjektivdeklination
Nominativ	e	Das sind **frische** Äpfel.	frisch**e** Äpfel
Akkusativ	e	Er verkauft **frische** Äpfel.	frisch**e** Äpfel
Dativ	en	Mit **frischen** Äpfeln kannst du Saft machen.	frisch**en** Äpfel**n**
Genitiv	er	Wie ist der Duft **frischer** Äpfel?	frisch**er** Äpfel

The endings are similar to the respective definite articles according to the case and gender except for masculine and neutral nouns of the Genitive case where the ending is 'en'.

7.3 Adjektivdeklination for nouns with indefinite articles

Following table shows endings that need to be added to the adjectives when an indefinite article is used.

	maskulin	feminin	neutrum	Plural
Nominativ	er	e	es	e
Akkusativ	en	e	es	e
Dativ	en	en	en	en
Genitiv	en	en	en	**er**

The endings as shown in the table above need to be added to the adjectives according to the gender, number and case of noun in the sentence. Examples are as follows.

maskulin

Case	ending	Example Sentence	Adjektivdeklination
Nominativ	er	Das ist ein **schneller** Zug.	ein schnell**er** Zug
Akkusativ	en	Ich sehe einen **schnellen** Zug.	einen schnell**en** Zug
Dativ	en	Ich möchte mit einem **schnellen** Zug reisen.	einem schnell**en** Zug
Genitiv	en	Wie ist der Weg eines **schnellen** Zuges?	eines schnell**en** Zuges

feminine

Case	ending	Example Sentence	Adjektivdeklination
Nominativ	e	Das ist eine **helle** Lampe.	eine hell**e** Lampe
Akkusativ	e	Ich kaufe eine **helle** Lampe.	eine hell**e** Lampe
Dativ	en	Mit einer **hellen** Lampe kann ich lesen.	einer hell**en** Lampe
Genitiv	en	Was ist die Farbe einer **hellen** Lampe?	einer hell**en** Lampe

neutrum

Case	ending	Example Sentence	Adjektivdeklination
Nominativ	es	Das ist ein **ruhiges** Hotel.	ein ruhig**es** Hotel
Akkusativ	es	Ich suche ein **ruhiges** Hotel.	ein ruhig**es** Hotel
Dativ	en	In einem **ruhigen** Hotel will ich bleiben.	einem ruhig**en** Hotel
Genitiv	en	Wie ist der Name eines **ruhigen** Hotels?	eines ruhig**en** Hotels

Plural

Case	ending	Example Sentence	Adjektivdeklination
Nominativ	e	Das sind **frische** Äpfel.	frisch**e** Äpfel
Akkusativ	e	Er verkauft **frische** Äpfel.	frisch**e** Äpfel
Dativ	en	Mit **frischen** Äpfeln kannst du Saft machen.	frisch**en** Äpfel**n**
Genitiv	**er**	Wie ist der Duft **frischer** Äpfel?	frisch**er** Äpfel

In the Nominative and Accusative cases the endings are similar to the definite articles. Except for the Genitive plural where the ending is **er**. For all other genders of Dative and Gentitive cases the endings are **en**.

7.4 Adjektivdeklination for nouns with definite articles

Following table shows endings that need to be added to the adjectives when a definite article is used.

	maskulin	feminin	neutrum	Plural
Nominativ	e	e	e	en
Akkusativ	en	e	e	en
Dativ	en	en	en	en
Genitiv	en	en	en	en

The endings as shown in the table above need to be added to the adjectives according to the gender, number and case of noun in the sentence. Examples are as follows.

maskulin

Case	ending	Example Sentence	Adjektivdeklination
Nominativ	e	Das ist der **schnelle** Zug.	der schnelle Zug
Akkusativ	en	Ich sehe den **schnellen** Zug.	den schnellen Zug
Dativ	en	Ich möchte mit dem **schnellen** Zug reisen.	dem schnellen Zug
Genitiv	en	Wie ist der Weg des **schnellen** Zuges?	des schnellen Zuges

feminine

Case	ending	Example Sentence	Adjektivdeklination
Nominativ	e	Das ist die **helle** Lampe.	die helle Lampe
Akkusativ	e	Ich kaufe die **helle** Lampe.	die helle Lampe
Dativ	en	Mit der **hellen** Lampe kann ich lesen.	der hellen Lampe
Genitiv	en	Was ist die Farbe der **hellen** Lampe?	der hellen Lampe

neutrum

Case	ending	Example Sentence	Adjektivdeklination
Nominativ	e	Das ist das **ruhige** Hotel.	das ruhige Hotel
Akkusativ	e	Ich suche das **ruhige** Hotel.	das ruhige Hotel
Dativ	en	In dem **ruhigen** Hotel will ich bleiben.	dem ruhigen Hotel
Genitiv	en	Wie ist der Name des **ruhigen** Hotels?	des ruhigen Hotels

Plural

Case	ending	Example Sentence	Adjektivdeklination
Nominativ	en	Das sind die **frischen** Äpfel.	die frischen Äpfel
Akkusativ	en	Er verkauft die **frischen** Äpfel.	die frischen Äpfel
Dativ	en	Mit den **frischen** Äpfeln kannst du Saft machen.	den frischen Äpfeln
Genitiv	en	Wie ist der Duft der **frischen** Äpfel?	der frischen Äpfel

The ending for nominative case singular and feminine and neutral genders in the accusative case is 'e'. For all other cases and the plural, the ending is 'en'.

7.5 Adjektivdeklination for nouns with negation and possessive articles

Following table shows endings that need to be added to the adjectives when negation and possessive articles is used.

	maskulin	feminin	neutrum	Plural
Nominativ	er	e	es	en
Akkusativ	en	e	es	en
Dativ	en	en	en	en
Genitiv	en	en	en	en

The endings as shown in the table above need to be added to the adjectives according to the gender, number and case of noun in the sentence. Examples are as follows.

maskulin

Case	ending	Example Sentence	Adjektivdeklination
Nominativ	er	Das ist kein **schneller** Zug.	kein schnell**er** Zug
Akkusativ	en	Ich sehe ihren **schnellen** Zug.	ihren schnell**en** Zug
Dativ	en	Ich möchte mit eurem **schnellen** Zug reisen.	eurem schnell**en** Zug
Genitiv	en	Wie ist der Weg seines **schnellen** Zuges?	seines schnell**en** Zuges

feminine

Case	ending	Example Sentence	Adjektivdeklination
Nominativ	e	Das ist keine **helle** Lampe.	keine hell**e** Lampe
Akkusativ	e	Ich kaufe seine **helle** Lampe.	seine hell**e** Lampe
Dativ	en	Mit meiner **hellen** Lampe kann ich lesen.	meiner hell**en** Lampe
Genitiv	en	Was ist die Farbe unserer **hellen** Lampe?	unserer hell**en** Lampe

neutrum

Case	ending	Example Sentence	Adjektivdeklination
Nominativ	es	Das ist kein **ruhiges** Hotel.	kein ruhig**es** Hotel
Akkusativ	es	Ich suche dein **ruhiges** Hotel.	dein ruhig**es** Hotel
Dativ	en	In Ihrem **ruhigen** Hotel will ich bleiben.	Ihrem ruhig**en** Hotel
Genitiv	en	Wie ist der Name seines **ruhigen** Hotels?	seines ruhig**en** Hotels

Plural

Case	ending	Example Sentence	Adjektivdeklination
Nominativ	en	Das sind keine **frischen** Äpfel.	keine frisch**en** Äpfel
Akkusativ	en	Er verkauft seine **frischen** Äpfel.	seine frisch**en** Äpfel
Dativ	en	Mit ihren **frischen** Äpfeln kannst du Saft machen.	ihren frisch**en** Äpfel**n**
Genitiv	en	Wie ist der Duft unserer **frischen** Äpfel?	unserer frisch**en** Äpfel

For singular, the endings are same as those used in indefinite articles while for plural, the endings are same as those used in definite articles.

8. Subjunctive (Konjunktiv II)

8.1 Concept of Konjunktiv II

In spoken as well as written German, politeness is considred to be a good trait. However looking at the basics of the German language, one can say that it is quite clear and straight forward without any hidden meanings behind words or phrases. French is largely used as a language of diplomacy due to its basic soft nature whereas German is the ideal language for technology due to its clarity of expression. However, there are certain situations where one has to sound polite in German in order to ensure the other person is not offended if adequate acquaintance has not been established yet.

The subjunctive form is the best to make the language polite. It is called as **Konjunktiv II** in German. There are many uses of Konjunktiv II like making polite requests or suggestions or advices or a wish and so on.

To give an analogy in English, consider the following sentences:

Can you please give me your phone number?

Could you please give me your phone number?

It can be clearly seen that on changing **Can** to **Could** the sentence sounds much more polite and courteous. It is to be noted that the <u>could</u> used here is in Present tense. Similarly in German, one uses the Konjunktiv II. Here as well, the Konjunktiv II is used in the present tense. The concept of using it to indicate the future is learnt at length at B1 and higher levels but at A2 the basics can be highly helpful to start with its use in day to day conversations.

8.2 Konjunktiv II for Modal Verbs

Modal verbs are the best to start learning Konjunktiv II because with them one can easily make requests. The following table provides the infinitive forms of the modal verbs and their Konjunktiv II forms.

Modalverb (Präsens)	Meaning	Modalverb (Konjunktiv II)	Meaning
dürfen	*allow*	dürften	*would allow*
können	*can*	könnten	*could*
mögen	*like*	möchten	*would like*
müssen	*must*	müssten	*would have to*
sollen	*should*	sollten	*should*
wollen	*want*	wollten	*wish to*

It can be seen that the Konjunktiv II forms are quite similar to the infinitive forms of the modal verbs in the Präsens. There is an additional **t** added before the 'en' ending. It can be seen that the modal verb **möchten** learnt at A1 is actually the Konjunktiv II of the modal verb mögen. The meanings given in the table are the nearest equivalents and should not be taken as direct translations. Refer the sentences given in the following sections to understand the meanings of the modal verbs in Konjunktiv II form.

Following table summarizes modal verbs in Konjunktiv II:

Präsens	dürfen	können	mögen	müssen	sollen	wollen
Konjunktiv II	**dürften**	**könnten**	**möchten**	**müssten**	**sollten**	**wollten**
ich	dürfte	könnte	möchte	müsste	sollte	wollte
du	dürftest	könntest	möchtest	müsstest	solltest	wolltest
er/sie/es	dürfte	könnte	möchte	müsste	sollte	wollte
wir	dürften	könnten	möchten	müssten	sollten	wollten
ihr	dürftet	könntet	möchtet	müsstet	solltet	wolltet
sie/Sie	dürften	könnten	möchten	müssten	sollten	wollten

The verb conjugation is done in a manner similar to the modal verbs conjugation pattern where the first and third person singular is conjugated similarly.

The following table provides sentences with the help of which one can understand the difference between the use of modal verbs in the present tense and as the subjunctive i.e. Konjunktiv II. The English equivalents are indicative only and not direct translations as the use of Konjunktiv II may intend to say something different in different contexts.

Präsens	Satz	Konjunktiv II	Satz
dürfen	Darf ich etwas sagen? *Am I allowed to say something?*	**dürften**	Dürfte ich etwas sagen? *Would I be allowed to say something?*
können	Kannst du mir einen Stift geben? *Can you give me a pen?*	**könnten**	Könntest du mir einen Stift geben? *Could you give me a pen?*
mögen	Mag er eine Pizza essen? *Does he like to eat Pizza?*	**möchten**	Möchte er eine Pizza essen? *Would he like to eat Pizza?*
müssen	Wir müssen pünktlich sein. *We must be on time.*	**müssten**	Wir müssten pünktlich sein. *We would have to be on time.*
sollen	Ihr sollt die Prüfung schreiben *You should write the exam*	**sollten**	Ihr solltet die Prüfung schreiben. *You should be writing the exam*
wollen	Sie wollen morgen ins Kino gehen. *They want to go to the cinema tomorrow*	**wollten**	Sie wollten morgen ins Kino gehen. *They wish to go to the cinema tomorrow.*

8.3 Difference between Konjunktiv II and Präteritum of Modal Verbs

Apart from the umlaut the basic difference between Konjunktiv II and Präteritum of modal verbs is the tense and intention. Konjunktiv II is always a polite way of asking or telling things in the present tense whereas Präteritum is used to report what happened using the simple past tense. The following table tries to summarize the infinitiv modal verb forms in Präsens, Präteritum and Konjunktiv II.

Modalverb (Präsens)	Meaning	Modalverb (Präteritum)	Meaning	Modalverb (Konjunktiv II)	Meaning
dürfen	*allow*	durften	*allowed to*	dürften	*would allow*
können	*can*	konnten	*could*	könnten	*could*
mögen	*like*	mochten	*liked*	möchten	*would like*
müssen	*must*	mussten	*had to*	müssten	*would have to*
sollen	*should*	sollten	*should have*	sollten	*should*
wollen	*want*	wollten	*wanted*	wollten	*wish to*

The following table provides a summary of use of these forms for a comprehensive comparative understanding of modal verbs as the case may be.

	Präsens Satz	Präteritum Satz	Konjunktiv II Satz
dürfen	**Darf** ich etwas sagen? *Am I allowed to say something?*	**Durfte** ich etwas sagen? *Was I allowed to say something?*	**Dürfte** ich etwas sagen? *Would I be allowed to say something?*
können	**Kannst** du mir einen Stift geben? *Can you give me a pen?*	**Konntest** du mir einen Stift geben? *Were you able to give me a pen?*	**Könntest** du mir einen Stift geben? *Could you give me a pen?*
mögen	**Mag** er eine Pizza essen? *Does he like to eat Pizza?*	**Mochte** er eine Pizza essen? *Did he like to eat Pizza?*	**Möchte** er eine Pizza essen? *Would he like to eat Pizza?*
müssen	Wir **müssen** pünktlich sein. *We must be on time.*	Wir **mussten** pünktlich sein. *We had to be on time.*	Wir **müssten** pünktlich sein. *We would have to be on time.*
sollen	Ihr **sollt** die Prüfung schreiben. *You should write the exam.*	Ihr **solltet** die Prüfung schreiben. *You should have written the exam.*	Ihr **solltet** die Prüfung schreiben. *You should be writing the exam.*
wollen	Sie **wollen** morgen ins Kino gehen. *They want to go to the cinema tomorrow.*	Sie **wollten** gestern ins Kino gehen. *They wanted to go to the cinema yesterday.*	Sie **wollten** morgen ins Kino gehen. *They wish to go to the cinema tomorrow.*

8.4 Konjunktiv II for sein, haben and other verbs

The verbs sein, haben and werden in their Präsens, Präteritum and Konjunktiv II infinitive forms can be summarized as follows.

	Präsens	Präteritum	Konjunktiv II
sein	sein	waren	wären
haben	haben	hatten	hätten
werden	werden	wurden	würden

The verb conjugation in Konjunktiv II is done in a manner similar to the modal verbs conjugation where the first and third person singular is the same. One of the uses of Konjunktiv II is to express wishes. One needs to know the Konjunktiv II form of only three verbs to express any kind of wish. The verbs **sein** and **haben** have their exclusive forms in the Konjunktiv II, while to express a wish considering any other verb, the Konjunktiv II form of the verb werden + Infinitiv is used. The following table provides a summary of use of these forms for a comprehensive comparative understanding. The English equivalents are indicative only and not direct translations as the use of Konjunktiv II.

	Präsens Satz	Präteritum Satz	Konjunktiv II Satz
sein	Er ist ein Ingenieur.	Er war ein Ingenieur.	Er wäre ein Ingenieur.
	He is an Engineer.	*He was an Engineer.*	*He would be an Engineer.*
haben	Ich habe einen Termin.	Ich hatte einen Termin.	Ich hätte einen Termin.
	I have an appointment.	*I had an appointment.*	*I would have an appointment.*
werden	Sie wird Brot essen.	Sie wurde Brot essen.	Sie würde Brot essen.
	She will eat bread.	*She was going to eat bread.*	*She would eat bread.*

Following table can be used as a reference. All other Verbs can be used in infinitive with conjugated form of würden to express wishes in a manner similar to the last example in the above table under Konjunktiv II with werden.

	sein	haben	All other verbs würden + Infinitiv
ich	wäre	hätte	würde
du	wärst	hättest	würdest
er/sie/es	wäre	hätte	würde
wir	wären	hätten	würden
ihr	wärt	hättet	würdet
sie/Sie	wären	hätten	würden

9. Compound Sentences

Till this point, one has come across only simple sentences. Simple sentences have only one Independent clause (Hauptsatz). At A2 level, one is introduced to Compound Sentences and Complex Sentences. Compound sentences contain two or more independent clauses joined by connectors called **co-ordinating conjunctions**. Complex sentences contain two or more dependent clauses and an independent clause joined by connectors called **subordinating conjunctions**. This chapter shall focus on Compound sentences while complex sentences shall be discussed at length in the chapters on Nebensätze and Relativsätze in this book.

9.1 The connector 'und'

The general sentence structure for a compound sentence using this connector is such that the first clause is written as it is. This is followed by the co-ordinate conjunction 'und' which is followed by the next independent clause. Both the clauses are written with their conjugated verbs in their second positions respectively.

Consider the following example:

Ich lese ein Buch und ich mag schreiben.

The format according to the above description with some more examples is explained as follows:

Compound Sentence	Hauptsatz 1	Konnektor	Hauptsatz 2
Ich lese ein Buch und ich mag schreiben.	Ich lese ein Buch	und	ich mag schreiben.
Sie kommt aus Indien und sie spricht Hindi.	Sie kommt aus Indien	und	sie spricht Hindi.
Wir essen Salat und wir trinken Cola.	Wir essen Salat	und	wir trinken Cola

In the sentences, the connector is written at Position 0 with respect to Hauptsatz 2 and the verbs in both the independent clauses are written at Position 2 in those respective clauses.

In Hauptsatz 2, one can omit writing the pronoun or verb if it is same as that of Hauptsatz 1. Thus the sentence may also be written as, "Ich lese ein Buch und ~~ich~~ mag schreiben."

9.2 The connector 'oder'

The general sentence structure for a compound sentence using this connector is such that the first clause is written as it is. This is followed by the co-ordinate conjunction 'oder' which is followed by the next independent clause. Both the clauses are written with their conjugated verbs in their second positions respectively.

Consider the following example:

Ich gehe ins Kino oder ich lese ein Buch.

The format according to the above description with some more examples is explained as follows:

Compound Sentence	Hauptsatz 1	Konnektor	Hauptsatz 2
Ich gehe ins Kino oder ich lese ein Buch.	Ich gehe ins Kino	oder	ich lese ein Buch.
Er lernt für die Prüfung oder er schläft heute Nacht.	Er lernt für die Prüfung	oder	er schläft heute Nacht.
Wir fahren nach Pune oder wir machen eine Grillparty.	Wir fahren nach Pune	oder	wir machen eine Grillparty.

In the sentences, the connector is written at Position 0 with respect to Hauptsatz 2 and the verbs in both the independent clauses are written at Position 2 in those respective clauses. In Hauptsatz 2, one can omit writing the pronoun or verb if it is same as that of Hauptsatz 1.

9.3 The connector 'aber'

The general sentence structure for a compound sentence using this connector is such that the first clause is written as it is. This is followed by a comma. The co-ordinate conjunction 'aber' is written right after the comma which is followed by the next independent clause. Both the clauses are written with their conjugated verbs in their second positions respectively.

Consider the following example:

Ich habe viele Termine, aber ich will arbeiten.

The format according to the above description with some more examples is explained as follows:

Compound Sentence	Hauptsatz 1	Konnektor	Hauptsatz 2
Ich habe viele Termine, aber ich will arbeiten.	Ich habe viele Termine,	aber	ich will arbeiten.
Er hatte Kopfschmerzen, aber er konnte fahren.	Er hatte Kopfschmerzen,	aber	er konnte fahren.
Wir mögen zu singen, aber wir tanzen jetzt.	Wir mögen zu singen,	aber	wir tanzen jetzt.

9.4 The connectors 'deshalb' and 'trotzdem'

In addition to the the frequently used connectors 'und, oder, aber' there are two more connectors used to express consequences or events that follow certain preceeding events. The connectors used are 'deshalb' and 'trotzdem'.

These are connectors used to indicate consequence of activities. Every activity definitely has a consequence. Depending on the perspective, it may be favourable or unfavourable. Sometimes, there may be contradictions as well. 'deshalb' is used as a connector to indicate a consequence i.e, Folge/Konsequenz and trotsdem is used to indicate a contradiction i.e. Widerspruch.

The structure of the new sentence formed is such that a comma is placed at the end of the first sentence (Hauptsatz 1). The connector deshalb / trotzdem is written after the comma with the conjugated verb of the second sentence written immediately after it. The subject takes the position right after the conjugated verb.

Thus the connector becomes a part of the second sentence (Hauptsatz 2) as it is written at Position 1 of Hauptsatz 2.

Consider the following example using the connector **deshalb**

Hauptsatz 1	Ich laufe jeder Morgen.	*I run everyday.*
Hauptsatz 2	Ich bin gesund.	*I am healthy.*
⇨	Ich laufe jeder Morgen, **deshalb** bin ich gesund.	*I run everyday; so I am healthy*

Consider the following example using the connector **trotzdem**

Hauptsatz 1	Ich trinke kein Bier.	*I don't drink beer.*
Hauptsatz 2	Ich muss zu der Party gehen.	*I have to go to the party.*
⇨	Ich trinke kein Bier, **trotzdem** muss ich zu der Party gehen.	*I don't drink beer, but still I have to go to the party.*

The English equivalents should not be taken as direct translations and are for reference only. In the above compound sentences, Hauptsatz 1 is written as it is. A comma is placed immediately after its end and the connector is written. Since the connector takes Position 1 in Hauptsatz 2, the conjugated verb is written immediately after the connector ar Position 2. This is followed by the subject and the rest of the sentence elements.

In the next two chapters Complex Sentences using subordinate and relative clauses have been explained at length.

10. Nebensätze (Complex Sentences with subordinate clause)

Till this point, only simple sentences were used to express anything in German. But at A2 level, it is expected that the user is able to give basic explainations and reasons for the statements made. This requires the ability to form complex sentences with a subordinate clause.

The word **Nebensatz** comprises of two words i.e. **neben** and **Satz** which literally means the next statement. This is called as the subordinate clause in English. Compound sentences with connectors like und, oder and so on have been introduced in the previous chapter. This chapter shall introduce Complex sentences with a subordinate clause.

A complex sentence is a combination of two sentences with a **subordinating** conjunction. A subordinate conjunction makes the attached clause dependent on the independent clause (Hauptsatz). Thus the combination of two sentences with a subordinate conjunction is called a Nebensatz i.e a complex sentence with a subordinate clause.

The general format of Nebensatz is as follows:

Hauptsatz 1 – comma (,) – subordinating conjunction – Nebensatz

z. B: <u>Ich lese Bücher, **weil** ich lesen **mag**</u>.

This has been explained as follows:

Position 1	Hauptsatz,	Ich lese Bücher,
Position 2	Subordinating conjunction	weil
Position 3	Nebensatz	ich lesen mag.

Hauptsatz refers to the Independent clause. This clause is followed by a comma. The subordinating conjunction is written immediately after the comma. Thereafter the subordinate clause is written. In German the subordinate clause is formed by writing the Hauptsatz with its conjugated verb at the end. This can be seen in the above example wherein the verb <u>mögen</u> is conjugated according to the person **ich** i.e <u>ich mag</u> and is written at the **end of the sentence**. Separable verbs are written in the conjugated form along with the prefix. All other elements that are generally written at the end of the sentence like Partizip II are written before this verb in Nebensatz. This has been elaborated at length in the following sections.

Following table summarizes the conjunctions for A2. The English equivalents given are indicative only and the meanings are the nearest expressions. Extensive examples have been given in the following sections to explain the concepts.

Subordinating Conjunction		Co-ordinating Conjunction	
weil	*because*	denn	*because*
obwohl	*eventhough*	und	*and*
dass	*that*	oder	*or*
als	*when*	aber	*but*
wenn	*if / when*		
damit	*in order to*		
um ... zu	*in order to*		

In the following sections, use of each of the subordinating conjunctions has been explained with the help of sentences. English equivalents have been avoided in order to make the reader capable of understanding the sentence formation in German itself as the nouns and verbs used have been learnt earlier. In case of doubts, the Appendix sections of this book and the book 'Let's Learn German A1' by the same author can be referred.

10.1 Nebensätze mit weil

Konnektor	weil	
Use	This subordinating conjunction is generally used to give a reason or justify something	
Simple Sentences	Satz 1	Ich lese Bücher
	Satz 2	Ich mag lesen.
	⇨	Ich lese Bücher, weil ich lesen **mag**.
With modal verb	Satz 1	Er ist müde.
	Satz 2	Er musste den ganzen Tag arbeiten.
	⇨	Er ist müde, weil er den ganzen Tag arbeiten **musste**.
With Perfekt	Satz 1	Sie ist müde.
	Satz 2	Sie hat seit einem Tag nicht geschlafen.
	⇨	Sie ist müde, weil sie seit einem Tag nicht geschlafen **hat**.
Nebensatz followed by Hauptsatz	Satz 1	Ich lese Bücher
	Satz 2	Ich mag lesen.
	⇨	Weil ich lesen **mag**, <u>lese</u> ich Bücher.

In all the complex sentences, the conjugated verb of the subordinate clause is written at the end of the sentence. When the subordinate clause is written first, the conjugated verb of the Independent clause is written right after the comma as seen underlined in the last example.

The conjunctions denn and weil are quite similar in meaning and can be used interchangeably to justify something. The only variation is in the sentence structure. If weil is used, the conjugated verb is written at the end of the <u>subordinate clause</u>. If denn is used, the conjugated verb is written in the second position in the <u>co-ordinate clause</u>.

A comparative example chart is as follows.

Denn-Sätze	Weil-Sätze
Ich trinke Cola, denn ich mag Cola.	Ich trinke Cola, weil ich Cola mag.
Ich will zu Haus gehen, denn ich möchte Pizza essen.	Ich will zu Haus gehen, weil ich Pizza essen möchte.
Kann ich ausgehen, denn ich hole meinen Freund ab.	Kann ich ausgehen, weil ich meinen Freund abhole.
Ich bin satt, denn ich habe so viel gegessen.	Ich bin satt, weil ich so viel gegessen habe.

Note: Separable verbs in Nebensatz are written at the end of the sentence in the conjugated form along with the prefix as can be seen in the third example above.

10.2 Nebensätze mit obwohl

Konnektor	obwohl	
Use	This subordinating conjunction is used to express contradiction between the independent clause and the subordinate clause. This implies that the subordinate clause gives a negative implication.	
Simple Sentences	Satz 1	Ich lese Bücher
	Satz 2	Ich mag schlafen.
	⇨	Ich lese Bücher, obwohl ich schlafen **mag**.
With modal verb	Satz 1	Er ist munter.
	Satz 2	Er musste den ganzen Tag arbeiten.
	⇨	Er ist munter, obwohl er den ganzen Tag arbeiten **musste**.
With Perfekt	Satz 1	Sie ist munter.
	Satz 2	Sie hat seit einem Tag nicht geschlafen.
	⇨	Sie ist munter, obwohl sie seit einem Tag nicht geschlafen **hat**.
Nebensatz followed by Hauptsatz	Satz 1	Ich lese Bücher
	Satz 2	Ich mag schlafen.
	⇨	Obwohl ich schlafen **mag**, <u>lese</u> ich Bücher.

In all the complex sentences, the conjugated verb of the subordinate clause is written at the end of the sentence. When the subordinate clause is written first, the conjugated verb of the Independent clause is written right after the comma as seen underlined in the last example.

10.3 Nebensätze mit dass

Konnektor	dass	
Use	This subordinating conjunction is generally used to give a reason or justify something	
Simple Sentences	Satz 1	Ich möchte sagen.
	Satz 2	Deutsch ist eine schöne Sprache.
	⇨	Ich möchte sagen, dass Deutsch eine schöne Sprache **ist**.
With modal verb	Satz 1	Er hat gesagt.
	Satz 2	Man muss mindestens eine Fremdsprache wissen.
	⇨	Er hat gesagt, dass man mindestens eine Fremdsprache wissen **muss**.
With Perfekt	Satz 1	Sie ist glücklich.
	Satz 2	Ihr Mann hat Zeit für sie gefunden.
	⇨	Sie ist glücklich, dass ihr Mann für sie Zeit gefunden **hat**.

In all the complex sentences, the conjugated verb of the subordinate clause is written at the end of the sentence.

Generally the subordinate clause is the direct object (Akkusativ) of the sentence if the verb in the first clause is denken, meinen, glauben usw. [2]

z.B: Ich glaube, dass er einen Laptop gekauft hat. (Laptop ist Akkusativ)

An indirect object added to the first clause makes it the Dative object.
z.B: Er hat mir gesagt, dass man mindestens eine Fremdsprache wissen muss. (mir ist Dativ und eine Fremdsprache ist Akkusativ)

At times there may be a need to add another clause after the subordinate clause. This secondary subordinate clause also follows the same structure wherein the conjugated verb is written in the last position. In the below example the conjugated Hilfsverb of the subordinate clauses in Perfekt has been written at the end of the respective clause. The co-ordinating conjunction und is used to combine the primary and secondary subordinate clauses.
z.B: Sie ist glücklich, dass ihr Mann für sie Zeit gefunden **hat** und ein schönes Geschenk gebracht **hat**.

An example using a subordinate conjunction between the primary and secondary subordinate clauses is as follows. It may be noted that a comma is marked before the secondary subordinating conjunction as well.
z.B: Sie ist glücklich, dass ihr Mann für sie Zeit gefunden **hat,** weil sie eine Überraschung **wollte**.

10.4 Nebensätze mit als

Konnektor	als	
Use	To describe an activity that took place **only once** in the past	
Simple Sentences	Satz 1	Ich lernte schwimmen.
	Satz 2	Ich war in der fünften Klasse.
	⇨	Ich lernte schwimmen, als ich in der fünften Klasse **war**.
With modal verb	Satz 1	Es war so komisch.
	Satz 2	Er musste vor uns tanzen.
	⇨	Es war so komisch, als er vor uns tanzen **musste**.
With Perfekt	Satz 1	Wir hatten viel Spaß.
	Satz 2	Wir sind nach Malvan gefahren.
	⇨	Wir hatten viel Spaß, als wir nach Malvan gefahren **sind**.
Nebensatz followed by Hauptsatz	Satz 1	Ich lernte schwimmen.
	Satz 2	Ich war in der fünften Klasse.
	⇨	Als ich in der fünften Klasse **war**, <u>lernte</u> ich schwimmen.

When the subordinate clause is written first, the conjugated verb of the Independent clause is written right after the comma as seen underlined in the last example.

10.5 Nebensätze mit wenn

Konnektor	wenn	
Use	To describe an activity that took place **multiple times** in the **past** or a <u>repetitive</u> event in the <u>present</u>	
Simple Sentences	Satz 1	Ich bin sehr glücklich.
	Satz 2	Ich lerne Deutsch.
	⇨	Ich bin sehr glücklich, wenn ich Deutsch **lerne**.
With modal verb	Satz 1	Ich bin sehr glücklich.
	Satz 2	Ich kann Deutsch lernen.
	⇨	Ich bin sehr glücklich, wenn ich Deutsch lernen **kann**.
With Perfekt	Satz 1	Ich bin sehr glücklich.
	Satz 2	Ich habe eine Stunde Deutsch gelernt.
	⇨	Ich bin sehr glücklich, wenn ich eine Stunde Deutsch gelernt habe.
Nebensatz followed by Hauptsatz	Satz 1	Ich bin sehr glücklich.
	Satz 2	Ich lerne Deutsch.
	⇨	Wenn ich Deutsch **lerne**, <u>dann</u> bin ich sehr glücklich

When the subordinate clause is written first, the particle <u>dann</u> is written right after the comma as seen underlined in the last example. This is followed by the conjugated verb of the independent clause.

10.6 Nebensätze mit damit und um ... zu

Konnektor	damit	
Use	To continue the sequence of events if the subject in the independent clause is <u>different</u> from that in the subordinate clause	
Simple Sentences	Satz 1	Ich gehe zu ihm.
	Satz 2	Er unterrichtet mir Deutsch.
	⇨	Ich gehe zu ihm, damit er mir Deutsch **unterrichtet**.
With modal verb	Satz 1	Ich gehe zu ihm.
	Satz 2	Er kann mir Deutsch unterrichten.
	⇨	Ich gehe zu ihm, damit er mir Deutsch unterrichten **kann**.
With Perfekt	Satz 1	Ich bin zu ihm gegangen.
	Satz 2	Er hat mir Deutsch unterrichtet.
	⇨	Ich bin zu ihm gegangen, damit er mir Deutsch unterrichtet **hat**.

The connector **damit** may also be used if the subject in the both the clauses is the same.

z.B: Er kommt zu mir, damit er mir Deutsch unterrichtet.

Konnektor	um ... zu	
Use	To continue the sequence of events if the subject in the independent clause is <u>same</u> as that in the subordinate clause	
Simple Sentences	Satz 1	Er kommt zu mir.
	Satz 2	Er unterrichtet mir Deutsch.
	⇨	Er kommt zu mir, **um** mir Deutsch **zu** unterrichten.
With modal verb	Satz 1	Er kommt zu mir.
	Satz 2	Er kann mir Deutsch unterrichten.
	⇨	Er kommt zu mir, **um** mir Deutsch unterrichten zu können.

A meaningful sentence in Perfekt cannot generally be formed.

The verb is written in zu + infinitive form at the end of the sentence.

For seperable verbs, the <u>zu</u> is written between the separable parts i.e. ein<u>zu</u>laden. Explaination is as follows:

Satz 1	Er schreibt mir.
Satz 2	Er lädt mich ein.
⇨	Er screibt mir, **um** mich ein**zu**laden

10.7 Indirekte Fragesatz

Asking indirect questions is considered to be a more polite way of seeking information than asking direct questions. That is to say, one can ask "Can I know where the car is?" rather than "Where is the car?"

10.7.1 Indirekte Fragesätze: W-Fragen

The structure of this type of Nebensatz remains the same as those with weil, dass usw. The independent clause is followed by a comma and then the subordinate clause is written. The W-Frage word is written immediately after the comma. However the way in which the subordinate clause is written is different from that written earlier. This is because, in these sentences one has to report what is happening or has happened. Thus the subordinate clause contains all pronouns in the <u>third person</u>. The verb of the subordinate clause is always conjugated in third person singular or plural and written at the end of the sentence. The conjugated verb of the subordinate clause may be a modal verb or separable verb as well depending on the sentence. Separable verb in the subordinate clause is written in the unseparated conjugated form at the end of the sentence. Following table provides a number of examples.

Direkte Fragen	Indirekte Fragesätze mit W-Fragen
Mann: **Wer** bist du?	Ein Mann hat ein anderer Mann gefragt, **wer** er ist.
Frau: **Was** kaufe ich für Abendessen ein?	Eine Frau hat meine Vermutung gefragt, **was** sie für Abendessen einkauft.
Kind: **Wo** kann ich etwas essen?	Das Kind fragt seine Mutter, **wo** es etwas essen kann.
Mann: **Woher** sind Sie gekommen?	Der Mann fragt eine Frau, **woher** sie gekommen ist.
Frau: **Wohin** hänge ich die Tafel?	Eine Frau fragt, **wohin** sie die Tafel hängt.
Kind: **Wie** schalte ich das Spielzeug ein?	Das Kind will wissen, **wie** es das Spielzeug einschaltet.
Mann: **Welche** Sprachen können Sie sprechen?	Der Mann fragt einen Taxifahrer, **welche** Sprachen er sprechen kann.
Frau: **Warum** ist der Salat nicht fertig?	Eine Frau will wissen, **warum** der Salat nicht fertig ist.
Kind: **Wann** kommt Pune?	Ein Kind fragt, **wann** Pune kommt.

10.7.2 Indirekte Fragesätze: Ja-/Nein-Fragen

The structure of this type of Nebensatz remains the same as that of the W-Fragen indirekte Fragesätze. The only change is that instead of the W-Frage, **ob** is written right after the comma. Following table illustrates the same examples in the Ja / Nein Fragen form.

Direkte Fragen	Indirekte Fragesätze mit Ja-/Nein-Fragen
Mann: Bist du Amit?	Ein Mann hat ein anderer Mann gefragt, **ob** er Amit ist.
Frau: Kaufe ich für Abendessen eine Gurke ein?	Eine Frau hat meine Meinung gefragt, **ob** sie für Abendessen eine Gurke einkauft.
Kind: Kann ich etwas essen?	Das Kind fragt seine Mutter, **ob** es etwas essen kann.
Mann: Sind Sie aus Indien gekommen?	Der Mann fragt eine Frau, **ob** sie aus Indien gekommen ist.
Frau: Hänge ich ein Bild an die Tafel?	Eine Frau fragt, **ob** sie ein Bild an die Tafel hängt.
Kind: Schalte ich das Spielzeug ein?	Das Kind will wissen, **ob** es das Spielzeug einschaltet.
Mann: Sprechen Sie Deutsch?	Der Mann fragt einen Taxifahrer, **ob** er Deutsch spricht.
Frau: Ist der Salat nicht fertig?	Eine Frau will wissen, **ob** der Salat nicht fertig ist.
Kind: Sind wir in Pune gekommen?	Ein Kind fragt, **ob** sie in Pune gekommen sind.

11. Relativsätze (Complex Sentences with relative clause)

Complex Sentences with subordinate clauses have been learnt in the previous chapter. This chapter shall introduce complex sentences with a relative clause. While the subordinate clause is used to justify the independent clause in a certain manner, the relative clause is used to relate the dependent clause with the independent clause. In Relativesätze, two claues are combined in such a way that a relation is established between the two by mentioning the subject with a relative pronoun. Generally the subordinate clause is dependent on the main clause. The independent clause introduces a subject and the direct object and the subordinate clause tells further about it by referring or relating to it.

The sentence structure for Relativesätze is such that the main clause is written as it is with a comma placed at its end. The relative pronoun is written right after the comma and the remaining part of the relative clause is written thereafter. The conjugated verb (modal/helping verb of Perfekt usw) is written at the end of this relative – subordinate clause. The relative pronouns need to be learnt separately for each case according to the gender and number. However if one is thorough with the definite articles, learning the relative pronouns is not a difficult task. The same have been summarized at the end of this chapter for ease of consolidation and revision.

The following sections provide details of relative pronouns for the four cases with examples. All varieties like modal verbs, Perfekt etc have been included. English equivalents have been avoided for comprehension of the sentence formation in German itself.

11.1 Relativsätze im Nominativ

For the Nominativ case, the relative pronouns used for Relativesätze are same as the definite articles for the Nominativ case i.e. **der, die, das, die**.

maskulin	der	Satz 1	Der Mann ist mein Freund.
		Satz 2	Er spricht Deutsch.
		⇨	Der Mann ist mein Freund, **der** Deutsch spricht.
feminin	die	Satz 1	Die Frau ist meine Freundin.
		Satz 2	Sie kauft einen Fisch ein.
		⇨	Die Frau ist meine Freundin, **die** einen Fisch einkauft.
neutrum	das	Satz 1	Das Kind ist mein Freund.
		Satz 2	Es muss ruhig sein.
		⇨	Das Kind ist mein Freund, **das** ruhig sein muss.
plural	die	Satz 1	Die Leute sind glücklich.
		Satz 2	Sie haben einen Schauspieler gesehen.
		⇨	Die Leute sind glücklich, **die** einen Schauspieler gesehen haben.

11.2 Relativsätze im Akkusativ

For the Akkusativ case, the relative pronouns used for Relativesätze are same as the definite articles for the Akkusativ case i.e. **den**, **die**, **das**, **die**.

maskulin	den	Satz 1	Der Mann ist mein Freund.
		Satz 2	Du fragst ihn.
		⇨	Der Mann ist mein Freund, **den** du fragst.
feminin	die	Satz 1	Die Frau ist meine Freundin.
		Satz 2	Du rufst sie an.
		⇨	Die Frau ist meine Freundin, **die** du anrufst.
neutrum	das	Satz 1	Das ist das Rathaus.
		Satz 2	Ich muss es besuchen.
		⇨	Das ist das Rathaus, **das** ich besuchen muss.
plural	die	Satz 1	Die Leute sind glücklich.
		Satz 2	Ich habe sie getroffen.
		⇨	Die Leute sind glücklich, **die** ich getroffen habe.

The above table has been prepared with sentences having accusative verbs. There may be situations where one may have to use prepositions that take the accusative case. In the following table examples of Relativsatz using accusative prepositions have been given. The overall sentence structure remains unchanged with a slight variation being that just before the relative pronoun, the preposition is written e.g: <u>für den</u> etc.

maskulin	den	Satz 1	Der Mann ist mein Freund.
		Satz 2	Ich arbeite für ihn.
		⇨	Der Mann ist mein Freund, für **den** ich arbeite.
feminin	die	Satz 1	Die Frau ist meine Freundin.
		Satz 2	Ich kaufe für sie ein.
		⇨	Die Frau ist meine Freundin, für **die** ich einkaufe.
neutrum	das	Satz 1	Das ist das Rathaus.
		Satz 2	Ich muss gegen es bleiben.
		⇨	Das ist das Rathaus, gegen **das** ich bleiben muss.
plural	die	Satz 1	Die Leute sind glücklich.
		Satz 2	Ich habe für sie gesungen.
		⇨	Die Leute sind glücklich, für **die** ich gesungen habe.

It can be seen that each relative clause thus establishes a relation with the independent clause and gives further information about it.

11.3 Relativsätze im Dativ

For the Dativ case, the relative pronouns used for Relativesätze for singular are same as the definite articles for the Dativ case i.e. **dem, der, dem**. For plural the relative pronoun is **denen**.

maskulin	dem	Satz 1	Der Mann ist mein Freund.
		Satz 2	Du dankst ihm.
		⇨	Der Mann ist mein Freund, **dem** du dankst.
feminin	der	Satz 1	Die Frau ist meine Freundin.
		Satz 2	Du sprichst ihr mit.
		⇨	Die Frau ist meine Freundin, **der** du mitsprichst.
neutrum	dem	Satz 1	Das ist das Kind.
		Satz 2	Ich muss ihm antworten.
		⇨	Das ist das Kind, **dem** ich antworten muss.
plural	denen	Satz 1	Die Leute sind glücklich.
		Satz 2	Ich habe ihnen gratuliert.
		⇨	Die Leute sind glücklich, **denen** ich gratuliert habe.

The above table has been prepared with sentences having dative verbs. There may be situations where one may have to use prepositions that take the dative case. In the following table examples of Relativsatz using dative prepositions have been given. The overall sentence structure remains unchanged with a slight variation being that just before the relative pronoun, the preposition is written e.g: <u>mit dem</u> etc.

maskulin	dem	Satz 1	Der Mann ist mein Freund.
		Satz 2	Ich arbeite mit ihm.
		⇨	Der Mann ist mein Freund, mit **dem** ich arbeite.
feminin	der	Satz 1	Die Frau ist meine Freundin.
		Satz 2	Ich kaufe bei ihr ein.
		⇨	Die Frau ist meine Freundin, bei **der** ich einkaufe.
neutrum	dem	Satz 1	Das ist das Rathaus.
		Satz 2	Ich muss vor ihm stehen.
		⇨	Das ist das Rathaus, vor **dem** ich stehen muss.
plural	denen	Satz 1	Die Leute sind glücklich.
		Satz 2	Ich habe mit ihnen gesungen.
		⇨	Die Leute sind glücklich, mit **denen** ich gesungen habe.

It can be seen that each relative clause thus establishes a relation with the independent clause and gives further information about it.

11.4 Relativsätze im Genitiv

For the Genitiv case, the relative pronouns used for Relativsätze are different from the definite articles and need to be known exclusively. They are **dessen**, **deren**, **dessen**, **deren**.

maskulin	dessen	Satz 1	Der Mann heißt Gourav.
		Satz 2	Sein Arbeitstisch ist weiß.
		⇨	Der Mann heißt Gourav, **dessen** Arbeitstisch weiß ist.
feminin	deren	Satz 1	Die Frau heißt Pooja.
		Satz 2	Ihr Konzert fängt am Abend an.
		⇨	Die Frau heißt Pooja, **deren** Konzert am Abend anfangt.
neutrum	dessen	Satz 1	Das Kind heißt Akshay.
		Satz 2	Sein Spielzeug musst du sehen.
		⇨	Das Kind heißt Akshay, **dessen** Spielzeug du sehen musst.
plural	deren	Satz 1	Die Leute sind glücklich.
		Satz 2	Ihr Urlaub hat gestern angefangen.
		⇨	Die Leute sind glücklich, **deren** Urlaub gestern angefangen hat.

11.5 Eingeschobene Relativsätze

The word **eingeschoben** literally means **inserted** and comes from the verb **einschieben** which means **to insert**. This is the next step in forming Relativesätze wherein, the relative clause is inserted into the independent clause to make the meaning clear by emphasizing on the relation established. The sentence structure for Eingeschobene Relativesätze is such that one phrase of the independent clause is written at first and a comma is put after it. The relative pronoun is written right after the comma which is followed by the relative clause. The conjugated verb (modal/heping verb of Perfekt usw) is written at the end of this relative - subordinate clause. Another comma is put right after its conjugated verb and the remaining phrase of the independent clause is written after it.

Following table gives the examples similar to the Nominativ case sentences (Sec 11.1)

maskulin	der	Satz 1	Der Mann ist mein Freund.
		Satz 2	Er spricht Deutsch.
		⇨	Der Mann, **der** Deutsch spricht, ist mein Freund.
feminin	die	Satz 1	Die Frau ist meine Freundin.
		Satz 2	Sie kauft einen Fisch ein.
		⇨	Die Frau, **die** einen Fisch einkauft, ist meine Freundin.
neutrum	das	Satz 1	Das Kind ist mein Freund.
		Satz 2	Es muss ruhig sein.
		⇨	Das Kind, **das** ruhig sein muss, ist mein Freund.
plural	die	Satz 1	Die Leute sind glücklich.
		Satz 2	Sie haben einen Schauspieler gesehen.
		⇨	Die Leute, **die** einen Schauspieler gesehen haben, sind glücklich.

Following tables give the examples similar to the Akkusativ case sentences (Sec 11.2)

maskulin	den	Satz 1	Der Mann ist mein Freund.
		Satz 2	Du fragst ihn.
		⇨	Der Mann, **den** du fragst, ist mein Freund.
feminin	die	Satz 1	Die Frau ist meine Freundin.
		Satz 2	Du rufst sie an.
		⇨	Die Frau, **die** du anrufst, ist meine Freundin.
neutrum	das	Satz 1	Das Rathaus ist bekannt.
		Satz 2	Ich muss es besuchen.
		⇨	Das Rathaus, **das** ich besuchen muss, ist bekannt.
plural	die	Satz 1	Die Leute sind glücklich.
		Satz 2	Ich habe sie getroffen.
		⇨	Die Leute, **die** ich getroffen habe, sind glücklich.

Akkusativ eingeschobene Relativsätze mit Prepositionen:

maskulin	den	Satz 1	Der Mann ist mein Freund.
		Satz 2	Ich arbeite für ihn.
		⇨	Der Mann, für **den** ich arbeite, ist mein Freund.
feminin	die	Satz 1	Die Frau ist meine Freundin.
		Satz 2	Ich kaufe für sie ein.
		⇨	Die Frau, für **die** ich einkaufe, ist meine Freundin.
neutrum	das	Satz 1	Das Rathaus ist groß.
		Satz 2	Ich muss gegen es bleiben.
		⇨	Das Rathaus, gegen **das** ich bleiben muss, ist groß.
plural	die	Satz 1	Die Leute sind glücklich.
		Satz 2	Ich habe für sie gesungen.
		⇨	Die Leute, für **die** ich gesungen habe, sind glücklich.

Following tables give the examples similar to the Dativ case sentences (Sec 11.3)

maskulin	dem	Satz 1	Der Mann ist mein Freund.
		Satz 2	Du dankst ihm.
		⇨	Der Mann, **dem** du dankst, ist mein Freund.
feminin	der	Satz 1	Die Frau ist meine Freundin.
		Satz 2	Du sprichst ihr mit.
		⇨	Die Frau, **der** du mitsprichst, ist meine Freundin.
neutrum	dem	Satz 1	Das Kind ist klug.
		Satz 2	Ich muss ihm antworten.
		⇨	Das Kind, **dem** ich antworten muss, ist klug.
plural	denen	Satz 1	Die Leute sind glücklich.
		Satz 2	Ich habe ihnen gratuliert.
		⇨	Die Leute, **denen** ich gratuliert habe, sind glücklich.

Dativ eingeschobene Relativsätze mit Prepositionen:

maskulin	dem	Satz 1	Der Mann ist mein Freund.
		Satz 2	Ich arbeite mit ihm.
		⇨	Der Mann, mit **dem** ich arbeite, ist mein Freund.
feminin	der	Satz 1	Die Frau ist meine Freundin.
		Satz 2	Ich kaufe bei ihr ein.
		⇨	Die Frau, bei **der** ich einkaufe, ist meine Freundin.
neutrum	dem	Satz 1	Das Rathaus ist groß.
		Satz 2	Ich muss vor ihm stehen.
		⇨	Das Rathaus, vor **dem** ich stehen muss, ist groß.
plural	denen	Satz 1	Die Leute sind glücklich.
		Satz 2	Ich habe mit ihnen gesungen.
		⇨	Die Leute, mit **denen** ich gesungen habe, sind glücklich.

Following tables give the examples similar to the Genitiv case sentences (Sec 11.4)

maskulin	dessen	Satz 1	Der Mann heißt Gourav.
		Satz 2	Sein Arbeitstisch ist weiß.
		⇨	Der Mann, **dessen** Arbeitstisch weiß ist, heißt Gourav.
feminin	deren	Satz 1	Die Frau heißt Pooja.
		Satz 2	Ihr Konzert fängt am Abend an.
		⇨	Die Frau, **deren** Konzert am Abend anfangt, heißt Pooja.
neutrum	dessen	Satz 1	Das Kind heißt Akshay.
		Satz 2	Sein Spielzeug musst du sehen.
		⇨	Das Kind, **dessen** Spielzeug du sehen musst, heißt Akshay.
plural	deren	Satz 1	Die Leute sind glücklich.
		Satz 2	Ihr Urlaub hat gestern angefangen.
		⇨	Die Leute, **deren** Urlaub gestern angefangen hat, sind glücklich.

11.6 Summary of Relativpronomen for all the cases

The relative pronouns for all the four cases can be summarized as follows. The ones different from the definite articles have been marked in bold.

	maskulin	feminin	neutrum	plural
Nominativ	der	die	das	die
Akkusativ	den	die	das	die
Dativ	dem	der	dem	**denen**
Genitiv	**dessen**	**deren**	**dessen**	**deren**

12. Everyday spoken and written German for A2

In the eleven chapters studied till this point, the grammar required for the A2 level has been covered along with examples given abundantly all over. In this chapter spoken and written German with respect to certain basic themes shall be studied. Refer the nouns tables in the Appendix section corresponding to these themes to build a strong vocabulary. The appendix also comprises of example sentences for the verbs at A2 level in alphabetical order.

Every section comprises of tables with certain generally asked questions and responses given. They are not related to each other and each pair tries to give an example of a certain concept learnt in Grammar in the previous chapters. Please note that the English meanings written in this chapter are only equivalent statements and not one to one translations of the German statements.

12.1 Socializing with people and pets

German Statement	English equivalent
F: Mit wem wollen Sie zum Abendessen kommen? A: Ich komme gerne mit meinen Eltern zum Abendessen.	*Q: With whom would you like to come for dinner?* *A: I would like to come with my parents for dinner.*
F: Kommst du nicht zum Restaurant? A: Doch. Ich komme gerne zum Restaurant.	*Q: Are you not coming to the Restaurant?* *A: I'm certainly coming to the Restaurant.*
F: Warum trinkst du kein Bier? A: Ich trinke kein Bier, weil ich es nicht mag.	*Q: Why don't you drink Beer?* *A: I don't drink it because I don't like it.*
F: Wer hat diesen Salat gemacht? A: Ich hatte mich heute Morgen ihn gemacht.	*Q: Who has made this salad?* *A: I have made it myself this morning.*
F: Könnten Sie mir bitte Ihre Handynummer geben? A: Ja, sicher. Sie ist 11 11 12 22 22.	*Q: Could you please give me your cell number?* *A: Yes surely. It is 11 11 12 22 22.*
F: Wann hast du fahren gelernt? A: Als ich 18 Jahre alt war, hatte ich fahren gelernt.	*Q: When have you learnt driving?* *A: I had learnt it when I was 18.*
F: Wann freust du dich? A: Ich freue mich, immer wenn meinen Hund zu mir kommt.	*Q: When are you happy?* *A: I'm happy everytime my dog comes to me.*

12.2 Academics and Education

German Statement	English equivalent
F: Konntest du in deiner Schule Pizza essen? A: Nein. Pizza und Pasta waren in der Schule verboten damals.	Q: Could you eat Pizza in your school? A: No. Pizza and pasta were prohibited back then in the school.
F: Wohin hast du die Bücher gelegen? A: Ich habe sie in den Schrank gelegen.	Q: Where have you placed the books? A: I have placed them in the closet.
F: Wo liegen die Bücher? A: Die Bücher liegen auf dem Tisch.	Q: Where are the books lying? A: The books aare lying on the table.
F: Warum hast du die Hausaufgabe nicht gemacht? A: Ich habe sie nicht gemacht, denn ich hatte keine Zeit für sie gefunden.	Q: Why have you not done the home-work? A: I did not do it because I didn't find time for it.
F: Warum hast du die Hausaufgabe nicht gemacht? A: Ich habe sie nicht gemacht, weil ich keine Zeit für sie gefunden hatte.	Q: Why have you not done the home-work? A: I did not do it because I didn't find time for it.
F: Wie sollte ich für den Sprachkurs anmelden? A: Sie sollten die Webseite besuchen und ein neues Formular einfüllen.	Q: How should I register for the language course? A: You should visit the website and fill up a new form.
F: Wessen Stift ist das? A: Das ist Gouravs Stift.	Q: Whose pen is this? A: This is Gourav's pen.

12.3 Fitness

German Statement	English equivalent
F: Warum bist du müde? A: Ich gehe jeder Morgen zu laufen, deshalb bin ich den ganzen Tag müde.	Q: Why are you tired? A: I run every morning; so I am tired all day.
F: Wie kannst du immer munter sein? A: Ich muss so viel arbeiten, trotzdem finde ich Zeit für Yoga, deshalb kann ich immer munter sein.	Q: How can you always be fresh? A: I must work a lot; however I find time for yoga; so I can always be fresh.
F: Kaufen Sie Obst für sich? A: Ja, ich kaufe sie gern für mich.	Q: Are you buying fruits for yourself? A: Yes I'm buying them for myself.
F: Wem möchten Sie für Ihre Gesundheit danken? A: Ich möchte meinem Yogalehrer danken. Er hat mich immer unterstützt.	Q: Who would you like to thank for your good health? A: I would like to thank my Yoga teacher. He has always supported me.

12.4 Being Professional

German Statement	English equivalent
F: Warum siehst du traurig? A: Na ja. Heute Morgen hatten wir ein langer Termin mit unserem Chef und er hat mir so viel in zwei kurze Tage zu tun gegeben!	*Q: What do you look sad?* *A: Nothing much. This morning we had a long meeting with the Boss and he has given me so much to do in two short days!*
F: Ohne wen gehst du zur Firma? A: Ich gehe ohne ihn.	*Q: Without whom do you go to the company?* *A: I go without him.*
F: Mit wem gehst du zur Firma? A: Ich gehe mit ihm.	*Q: With whom do you go to the company?* *A: I go with him.*
F: Wann hat unseren Mitarbeiter Geburtstag? Wie alt wird er? A: Er hat am 30. Juli Geburtstag und wird 27.	*Q: When does our co-worker have birthday? How old will he be?* *A: He has birthday on 30th July and is turning 27.*

12.5 On the go!

German Statement	English equivalent
F: Wie findest du dein Auto? A: Ich finde es praktisch. Es ist so teuer wie das Auto meines Freundes, aber läuft schneller als sein Auto.	*Q: How do you find your car?* *A: It is practical. It is as expensive as my friend's car but runs faster.*
F: Welcher Zug kann ich nach Pune nehmen? Was emphiehlst du? A: Ich glaube, dass Zug 111 ist gut, aber er ist so gut wie Zug 222 beim Pünktlichkeit. Zug 333 ist besser als 222, weil er immer pünktlich ist. Du kannst auch Zug 444 nehmen. Er ist am besten, weil die Karten sind billiger als alle andere Züge und er kommt nie spät.	*Q: Which train can I take to Pune? What do you recommend?* *A: I think Train 111 is good but it is as good as Train 222 with punctuality. Train 333 is better than 222 because it is always on time. You may also take Train 444. It is the best because the tickets are cheaper compared to others and it never comes late.*
F: Was ist passiert? Was will der Mann wissen? A: Er will wissen, warum der Zug spät kommt.	*Q: What happened? What does the man want to know?* *A: He wants to know why the train is late.*

12.6 Exploring cities and Travel

German Statement	English equivalent
F: Was für ein Urlaub wollen Sie machen? A: Wir wollen einen Campingurlaub bei dem Strand machen.	*Q: What kind of tour do you want to do?* *A: We want to do a camping tour at the beach.*
F: Ist jemand dort gegangen? A: Ja. Mein Onkel ist dort letzter Monat besuchen.	*Q: Has anyone been there?* *A: Yes. My uncle had been there last month.*

German Statement	English equivalent
F: Wen möchten Sie im Urlaub besuchen? A: Wir besuchen meinen Bruder, den ich letztes Jahr getroffen habe.	*Q: Whom are you visiting in the tour? A: We are visiting my brother, whom I had met last year.*

12.7 Expressing yourself

German Statement	English equivalent
F: Worüber ärgerst du dich? Über die Verspätung deines Freunds? A: Ja, darüber.	*Q: What are you angry about? Is it the delay of your friend? A: Yes about that.*
F: Worüber machst du dir Sorge? A: Ich warte hoffentlich auf das Prüfungsergebnis und mache mir Sorge darüber.	*Q: What are you worrying about? A: I'm waiting hopefully for the exam results and am worrying about that.*

12.8 General points [1] [2]

- In German, there are many verb pairs that are similar with a minor variation in meaning like laufen – rennen, wissen – kennen, studieren - lernan usw. It can be explained as: Wir **wissen** etwas, aber wir **kennen** jemand. Wir **studieren** einen Kurs, aber wir **lernen** für eine Prüfung.

- Generally all nouns ending with **ung / keit / heit** are feminine and their plural ends with **en**

- To express quantity following adjectives are used.

  viel ~ much (not countable)   mehrere ~ several (not countable)

  viele ~ many (countable)   mehr ~ more (countable)

- In German, one works <u>at the place of</u> somebody/something i.e. Ich arbeite **bei** VW.

- To thank someone for their precious time, one can say, **Vielen Dank für Ihre Aufmerksamkeit**.

- *What a pleasant surprise!* ~ Eine angenehme Überrashung!

- For prepositions zu und nach, zu is used to refer to something local in the city like 'Ich gehe zum Rathaus' while nach is used to refer to something outside like 'Ich gehe nach Pune'. An exception (e Ausnahme, -n) is Ich gehe <u>nach</u> Hause.

- The infinitive of the verb can be used as a noun with the article das. i.e. kochen - das Kochen (Singular),

- Nouns indicating names of animals can be added with suffixes –chen and –lein to make nouns for their young ones. The new nouns thus formed are always Neuter

- The positive reply to a phrase with a reflexive verb like ‚Ich freue mich' is generally ‚Ich mich auch' while the negative would be ‚Ich mich leider nicht!'

- The positive reply to a phrase with a reflexive verb like ‚Ich freue mich' is generally ‚Ich mich auch' while the negative would be ‚Ich mich leider nicht!'

13. Goethe Zertifikat A2 Exam

In this chapter the details of Goethe German A2 Exam have been given. Every section contains information on certain skills required, conduct and points to remember for the specific modules and parts therein.

A summary of the Goethe Zertifikat A2 Prüfung is as follows [1][7]:

Teil	Section	Marks	Duration	Conduct
1	Lesen (*Reading*)	25	30 min	Individual
2	Hören (*Listening*)	25	30 min	Individual
3	Schreiben (*Writing*)	25	30 min	Individual
4	Sprechen (*Speaking*)	25	15 min	Group
Total		100	105 min	

Total marks = 100

Passing marks = 60 (15 für Sprechen + 45 zusammen für Lesen, Hören und Schreiben)

The four sections viz. Lesen, Hören, Schreiben and Sprechen carry 25 marks each. The first three are conducted in quick succession in a room where one is given the question booklet and answer sheet and the correct answers have to be crossed on it accordingly. The Sprechen module is conducted separately after a brief break in another room.

The minimum passing marks for the exam are 60. But it is important to note that for A2, the candidate has to score a minimum of 15 marks in Sprechen and 45 in the other three parts to pass the exam. This implies that if the candidate scores 14 marks in Sprechen and 46 in Lesen, Hören and Schreiben, although the total is 60, the candidate is marked to have failed the exam. Thus it is important to practise speaking German at least to yourself if not with others. Section-wise details of the exam are as follows:

Teil 1: Lesen

Teil	Details	Questions	Marks
1.1	1 Article and related questions Answer is 'A' or 'B' or 'C'	5	5
1.2	Pamplets or Brochures or Lists Answer is 'A' or 'B' or 'C'	5	5
1.3	E-Mail Answer is 'A' or 'B' or 'C'	5	5
1.4	People and related advertisements Match the advertisements	5	5
Total		20	20

Total 20 questions = 20 marks

20 marks * 1.25 = 25 marks

Teil 2: Hören

Teil	Details	Questions	Marks
2.1	5 audios each played twice Answer is 'A' or 'B' or 'C'	5	5
2.2	1 Dialogue with a variety of information played once Identify the activity and choose the correct picture	5	5
2.3	5 Audios each played once Identify the activity and mark the correct picture Answer is 'A' or 'B' or 'C'	5	5
2.4	1 Interview between two people Answer is 'Ja' or 'Nein' / 'Richtig' or 'Falsch'	5	5
	Total	20	20

Total 20 questions = 20 marks

20 marks * 1.25 = 25 marks

Teil 3: Schreiben

Teil	Details	Questions	Marks
3.1	Write an informal SMS to your friend in 20 to 30 words	1	10
3.2	Write a Formal E-Mail in 30 to 40 words	1	10
	Total	2	20

Total 2 questions = 20 marks

20 marks * 1.25 = 25 marks

Teil 4: Sprechen

Teil	Details	Marks
4.1	4 Cards with some words written on it (With Partner) 4 Questions to be asked and answered and vice versa	4
4.2	Mini Presentation (Individial) Card with a theme and 4 helping words/phrases given Speak at least two sentences on each	8
4.3	Plan something together (With Partner) You and Partner have to decide on something	8
	Overall Pronunciation (Aussprache)	5
	Total	25

The Points and respective Ratings for the exam are as follows:

Points	Rating	
100 - 90	sehr gut	Very Good
89 - 80	gut	Good
79 - 70	befriedigend	Satisfactory
69 - 60	ausreichend	Average
59 - 0	nicht bestanden	Fail

In the following sections, each part has been elaborated with necessary details for the candidates. Examination preparation material can be obtained from the official website of the Goethe Institute. Model answers of the Schreiben part have also been given there.

13.1 Lesen

Lesen is the first module in the Goethe Zertifikat A2 examination. The candidate is required to read the questions given in the booklet and mark the correct answer on the answer sheet individually. Following tables elaborate the four sub-modules of this module.

1.1 An Article and related questions
What has to be done in the exam?
An article that can be generally found in a Newspaper is given and questions are asked based on the text given therein. The text length is around 200 words. There are five questions asked and each question is given with three choices out of which one is correct. The correct answer has to be crossed.
What are the skills required?
• Ability to skim through text and mentally note the keywords • Ability to understand the intonation of the questions • Ability to deduce simple meanings from the questions and statements
Tips and other information
• Read the questions first and try to search the related information in the text • The questions are generally given serially i.e. the information in the text can be found in the same order as that of the questions • Answer the questions only with respect to the information given. Do not assume any information yourself

1.2 Pamplets or Brochures or Lists in a store

What has to be done in the exam?

There is an information pamplet given with the location of various items in a store. One has to read the question and choose the correct option where the given item can be found. This is like looking for the floor or room in which the required item can be found. Five questions with three options each are given. The correct answer has to be crossed.

What are the skills required?

- Ability to orient oneself in a store
- Ability to read information boards and locate items
- Ability to group items based on their nature
- Ability to identify unwanted information and eliminate the same

Tips and other information

- Read the question first and understand the item required
- Read the options given and check the possibility of each
- It may happen that none of the mentioned rooms/locations have the required item. In that case there generally an option which says that the item is in some other hall or location. This option has to be marked as the correct answer

1.3 E-Mail

What has to be done in the exam?

An E-mail (formal or semi-formal) has to be read. Five questions are asked with three options each. The correct option has to be crossed.

What are the skills required?

- Ability to extract required information from the text
- Ability to understand the intonation of the text and the intention behind it
- Ability to distinguish the sender from the receiver

Tips and other information

- In this task also the sequence of questions and the information in the text is same
- Do not read the entire E-mail first
- Read the question first and try to figure out the answer by refering the specific part of the text

1.4 Matching advertisements and people's requirements

What has to be done in the exam?

There are six advertisements given in the exam and requirements of five different people in the form of five questions. One has to choose the most suitable adverstisement for the person and mark the correct option. This implies there is only one advertisement that completely matches the requirements of the person. One of the requirements / situation has no suitable advertisement. That has to be marked with an X as instructed.

What are the skills required?

- Ability to understand requirements and find an appropriate solution

Tips and other information

- Ensure the option chosen suits all the requirements. There are generally two advertisements with similar requirements. Do not choose the answer in a hurry

13.2 Hören

Hören is the second module in the Goethe Zertifikat A2 examination. The candidate is required to listen to the audios played in the examination hall and mark the correct answer on the answer sheet for the question asked individually. Following tables elaborate the four sub-modules of this module.

2.1 Understanding announcements and instructions for public
What has to be done in the exam?
Five audios are played and each has a question to be answered based on it. Choose the correct answer among three options.
What are the skills required?
<ul><li>Ability to pick up information from announcements</li><li>Ability to filter necessary and unnecessary information with respect to the context</li></ul>
Tips and other information
<ul><li>Each audio is played twice. In the first run, try to finalyse the answer. In the second run, confirm it</li><li>All the options may be spoken out in the audio but only one is correct with reference to the question</li><li>The audios are played one after the other with a gap of around 15 seconds given to read the question</li></ul>

2.2 Understanding a dialogue with a time table
What has to be done in the exam?
A dialogue between two people is played in the exam. The dialogue is such that it gives a time table of activities to be done or have been done on various days or time slots. Nine pictures are given out of which five are correct. The correct picture has to be chosen against the day or time asked in the time table. One example is played first and then the dialogue is played at once.
What are the skills required?
<ul><li>Ability to grasp pictorial and audio information simultaneously</li><li>Ability to filter important or required information from the dialogue</li><li>Ability to handle variety of information</li></ul>
Tips and other information
<ul><li>The audio is played once only</li><li>See all the pictures before the actual dialogue starts</li><li>Try to figure out the verbs and nouns that can be associated with the pictures before the dialogue starts</li><li>Try to make a mind map of the information given in the pictures</li><li>Out of 9 options, one is already marked in the example; 5 are marked with the help of the dialogue and 3 are extra</li><li>All the options may be spoken out in the dialogue but there may be words like kein or nicht that makes it easy to eliminate the incorrect ones</li></ul>

- If a particular point is missed, go to the next part of the dialogue and avoid pondering over the previous question as the recording is played only once

---

2.3 Choose the correct picture by listening to the audio

What has to be done in the exam?

Five audios are played once, one after the other. Each audio has a question based on it with three options given in the form of pictures. Listen to the audio and choose the correct picture that answers the question.

What are the skills required?

- Ability to grasp pictorial and audio information simultaneously
- Ability to differentiate between minute aspects of speech

Tips and other information

- The audios are each played only once
- All the options may be heard in the audio but only one of them is the correct answer.
- The speed of these audios is generally fast. Hence it is good to be attentive to all the relevant information

---

2.4 Understanding an Interview on Radio

What has to be done in the exam?

There is a dialogue played twice. Based on the information in the dialogue, five statements are made and one has to mark whether the statement made is correct or otherwise.

What are the skills required?

- Ability to simultaneously understand written and audio information
- Ability to make an instant decision whether whatever was heard has been written

Tips and other information

- The audio is played as a dialogue twice. This means the entire dialogue is played twice and not the parts. In the first run, try to finalyse the answers. In the second run, confirm them
- The speed of the dialogue is generally fast
- Move to the next statement if the track of the previous statement was lost
- Stay attentive during this sub-module as information may be spoken out quickly

In the examination, the candidates are made to sit in a sufficiently sound-proof room in order to understand the audios better. There are no disturbances of any kind. The invigilator carries out a sound check to ensure all the candidates sitting in the room are able to follow the audio at ease. The Hören exam is such that the candidate has to simultaneously read the question and options and listen to the audio. This test is more of a test of comprehension of spoken German than a mere listening test. Once the audio starts, there is no break given in between. However there are sufficient pauses of 10 to 15 seconds given between the questions to read the same. This can help the candidate anticipate certain flow of information of the audio. For the A2 level, the pace of the dialogues and audios is faster as compared to that heard in A1. This implies one should get acquainted with a higher version of spoken German while giving the A2 exam which can be easily done with practise.

13.3 Schreiben

Schreiben is the third module in the Goethe Zertifikat A2 examination. The candidate is required to write two texts according to the instructions given. Following tables elaborate the two sub-modules of this module.

3.1 To write an SMS
What has to be done in the exam?
An SMS has to be written using the 3 points mentioned in 20 - 30 words
What are the skills required?
<ul><li>Knowledge of informal salutations</li><li>Ability to ask questions</li><li>Ability to give reasons using subordinate clause</li></ul>
Tips and other information
<ul><li>Write the SMS in informal **du** form</li><li>Write the salutations accordingly</li><li>Names of persons should not be written. Instead write ABC as your name</li><li>Ensure all the three points are addressed</li></ul>

3.2 To write an E-Mail
What has to be done in the exam?
An E-Mail has to be written using the 3 points mentioned in 30 - 40 words
What are the skills required?
<ul><li>Basic knowledge of E-Mail format learnt at A1 level</li><li>Knowledge of formal salutations</li><li>Ability to ask questions</li><li>Ability to give reasons using subordinate clause</li></ul>
Tips and other information
<ul><li>Write the E-Mail in formal **Sie** form</li><li>Write the salutations accordingly</li><li>Names of persons should not be written. Instead use ABC or XYZ</li><li>Ensure all the three points are addressed</li></ul>

The Schreiben module is the most scoring module. One can easily score full marks if the text written is free from spelling mistakes, grammatical errors and answers all the three points mentioned in the question booklet are addressed.

There is a general tendency that we like cleanliness. Hence the text written in exam answer sheet should be written neatly with a legible handwriting. The total time given is 30 minutes. It is good if the structure is mentally thought of before starting to write. If permitted during the exam, the candidate may even practise writing on the question booklet and write the final answer on the answer sheet. Time management thus becomes an important aspect. Sufficient practice can help one score full marks in this module.

13.4 Sprechen

Sprechen is the fourth module in the Goethe Zertifikat A2 examination. The candidate is required to carry out discussions and speak about a topic with certain helping words. This exam is conducted in a room with two examiners and one other candidate. No fifth person would generally be there in the room. This module has to be passed separately with at least 15 marks. Following tables elaborate the three sub-modules of this module.

4.1 Knowing each other in an informal conversation
What has to be done in the exam?
Four cards with a word written on each of them are given to each of the two candidates. A question has to be formed with the help of these words. The other candidate (partner) has to be asked this question and then they are required to reply in at least two sentences. The partner then formulates four questions and asks them and you are required to similarly answer them in at least two sentences.
What are the skills required?
<ul><li>Ability to understand the intonation of the question</li><li>Ability to form questions on the spot</li><li>Ability to understand and respond to a question</li><li>Ability to give reasons with the help of subordinate clause</li></ul>
Tips and other information
<ul><li>Ask the questions in a sentence only. Do not make it too long or too short</li><li>Ask the questions using the **du** form for a better informal ambience</li><li>Try to use different sentence structures like Perfekt, modal verbs etc</li><li>Answer the question always with a reason. This can be done easily using Nebensatz</li></ul>

4.2 Mini Presentation on a general topic
What has to be done in the exam?
A card with a Theme of general interest is given to the candidate. The card has a central theme written on it with four related words written around it. The candidate has to speak about themselves by adhering to the theme using the helping words. At the end, the examiner may ask one or two further questions on the theme.
What are the skills required?
<ul><li>Ability to speak on a topic as an extempore</li><li>Ability to formulate sentences with given helping words</li></ul>
Tips and other information
<ul><li>This is a test of your ability to understand a theme and speak about it without special preparation</li><li>Speak clearly with proper intonation as pronunciation carries marks</li><li>Any additional words other than those mentioned on the card can also be spoken and it is not necessary that all the given words have to be touched</li><li>Do not speak in too small sentences. Make use of Nebensatz or Relativsatz to make the sentences longer</li><li>Use different types of sentence structures</li></ul>

4.3 Planning something with your partner

What has to be done in the exam?

This is the most interesting part of Sprechen module where actual interaction takes place. Both the candidates receive a card each with a time table written on it. It is required that the candidates do not see each other's cards during the test. There is a situation given in the form of a question and the candidates need to discuss and find a suitable time according to the time tables given to them. There are certain time slots when both may be busy and a few when either of them may be busy. The aim is to discuss and finalise a time when both are free for the task.

What are the skills required?

- Ability to understand time and activities
- Ability to give reason for being busy. The cards have the reason written in short. The candidate has to form a sentence using it with Nebensatz
- Ability to give suggestions about another time
- Ability to respond politely to the suggestions

Tips and other information

- Use the informal **du** form to make the conversation lively
- Speak clearly with proper intonation as pronunciation carries marks
- Answer in longer sentences with Nebensatz. If you have an activity mentioned at the time asked by the partner, give reason using the name of that activity
- Use Redemittel like Geht es um ...? to ask whether they are free at a given time where no activity is mentioned in your card
- Try to find the best time when both are free i.e. no activity is mentioned at that time in each other's cards
- Conclude the conversation by confirming the time and place of meeting and anything to be taken along

The Sprechen Test has 5 marks exclusively for the pronunciation. When learning German as a foreign language, it is natural to get a regional accent mixed with it. This can be overcome by listening to native German speakers on a regular basis and trying to speak yourself.

The next question comes, who to talk to if there is nobody. The best way in this case is to talk to yourself. Start with simple sentences and build a castle of your own imagination in German. It sounds funny at first but is the best way to practise speaking.

Complete exam material including Hören audios is available for download on the official website of the Goethe Institut. The reader can get the same from there for exam preparation.

Appendix

Appendix 1. List of new Nouns for A2

Ap.1 Socializing with people and pets

Masculine Nouns from this theme for A2					
Singular (der)	**Plural (die)**	**Meaning**	**Singular (der)**	**Plural (die)**	**Meaning**
Affe	Affen	*Monkey*	Müll	-	*Garbage*
Bär	Bären	*Bear*	Polizist	Polizisten	*Police officer*
Bauernhof	Bauernhöfe	*Farm*	Rauch	-	*Smoke*
Beutel	Beutel	*Handbag*	Rückweg	Rückwege	*Return-way*
Briefkasten	Briefkästen	*Letter box*	Schritt	Schritte	*Step*
Brunnen	-	*Fountain*	Schwan	Schwäne	*Swan*
Dichter	Dichter	*Poet*	Sinn	Sinne	*Sense*
Eindruck	Eindrücke	*Impression*	Stadttrand	Stadtränder	*Outskirts*
Eingang	Eingänge	*Input*	Stein	Steine	*Stone*
Einwohner	Einwohner	*Resident*	Stil	Stile	*Style*
Gastraum	Gasträume	*Guest room*	Stoffbeutel	Stoffbeutel	*Bag*
Gedanke	Gedanken	*Thought*	Storm	-	*Storm*
Gegenstand	Gegenstände	*Object*	Strand	Strände	*Beach*
Geruch	Gerüche	*Odour*	Tierarzt	Tierärzte	*Veteniary*
Hase	Hasen	*Rabbit*	Tiger	Tiger	*Tiger*
Haushalt	Haushalte	*Household*	Umzug	Umzüge	*Move*
Kinderwagen	Kinderwagen	*Stroller*	Unterschied	Unterschiede	*Difference*
Kleber	Kleber	*Glue*	Vogel	Vögel	*Bird*
Kochkurs	Kochkurse	*Cook-course*	Vorraum	Vorräume	*Ante-room*
Konflikt	Konflikte	*Conflict*	Zaun	Zäune	*Fence*
Mitstudent	Mitstudenten	*Co-student*	Zitronensaft	Zitronensäfte	*Lemon Juice*

Feminine Nouns from this theme for A2					
Singular (die)	**Plural (die)**	**Meaning**	**Singular (die)**	**Plural (die)**	**Meaning**
Ausnahme	Ausnahmen	*Exception*	Kerze	Kerzen	*Candle*
Bohne	Bohnen	*Bean*	Kuh	Kühe	*Cow*
Dauer	-	*Duration*	Ordnung	-	*Order*
Eigenschaft	Eigenschaften	*Characteristic*	Pfanne	Pfannen	*Pan*
Einführung	Einfürungen	*Introduction*	Ratte	Ratten	*Rat*
Ente	Enten	*Duck*	Schildkröte	Schildkröten	*Turtle*
Fläche	Flächen	*Surface*	Verneinung	Verneinungen	*Negation*

Haustür	Haustüren	*House-door*	Wiederholung	Wiederholungen	*Revision*
Insel	Inseln	*Island*	Wolke	Wolken	*Cloud*

Neutral Nouns from this theme for A2					
Singular (das)	Plural (die)	Meaning	Singular (das)	Plural (die)	Meaning
Bonbon	Bonbons	*Sweets*	Gute	-	*Quality*
Boot	Boote	*Boat*	Haustier	Haustiere	*Pet*
Dach	Dächer	*Roof*	Licht	Lichter	*Light*
Dorf	Dörfer	*Village*	Päckchen	Päckchen	*Parcel*
Dunkle	-	*Dark*	Rad	Räder	*Wheel*
Ergebnis	Ergebnisse	*Result*	Schwein	Schweine	*Pig*
Erlebnis	Erlebnisse	*Adventure*	Sieb	Siebe	*Sieve*
Feuer	-	*Fire*	Tierheim	Tierheime	*Shelter*
Gedicht	Gedichte	*Poem*	Ufer	Ufer	*Riverbank*
Geschirr	-	*Dishes*			

Ap.2 Academics and Education

Masculine Nouns from this theme for A2					
Singular (der)	Plural (die)	Meaning	Singular (der)	Plural (die)	Meaning
Abschluss	Abschlüsse	*Conclusion*	Prüfer	Prüfer	*Examiner*
Alterpfleger	Alterpfleger	*Care-taker*	Ratschlag	Ratschläge	*Advice*
Arme	Armen	*Poor*	Riesenspaß	-	*Fun*
Auftrag	Aufträge	*Order*	Schlaf	-	*Sleep*
Beitrag	Beiträge	*Article*	Spiegel	Spiegel	*Mirror*
Besuch	Besuche	*Visit*	Steckbrief	Steckbriefe	*Features*
Eintrag	Einträge	*Entry*	Stoff	-	*Material*
Fehler	Fehler	*Error*	Stundenplan	Stundenpläne	*Study-plan*
Forumstext	Forumstexte	*Information*	Tagesablauf	Tagesabläufe	*Schedule*
Hauptteil	Hauptteile	*Gist*	Wert	-	*Worth*
Hotelkaufmann	Hotelkaufmänner	*Hotel-seller*	Zeitplan	Zeitpläne	*Time-table*
Lokführer	Lokführer	*Train-pilot*	Zuhörer	Zuhörer	*Listener*

Feminine Nouns from this theme for A2					
Singular (die)	Plural (die)	Meaning	Singular (die)	Plural (die)	Meaning
Ablenkung	Ablenkungen	*Diversion*	Gewohnheit	Gewohnheiten	*Habit*
Ausbildung	Ausbildungen	*Training*	Gliederung	Gliderungen	*Outline*
Austellung	Austellungen	*Exhibition*	Grippe	Grippen	*Flu*
Checkliste	Checklisten	*Checklist*	Karriere	-	*Career*
Disziplin	-	*Discipline*	Oper	Opern	*Opera*
Einleitung	Einleitungen	*Initiation*	Reportage	Reportagen	*Report*
Erholung	-	*Recreation*	Untersuchung	Untersuchungen	*Examination*

Erinnerung	Erinnerungen	*Reminder*	Veränderung	Veränderungen	*Change*
Frucht	Früchte	*Fruit*	Vorbereitung	Vorbereitungen	*Preparation*
Gehörlose	Gehörlosen	*Deaf*	Vorlesung	Vorlesungen	*Lecture*

Neutral Nouns from this theme for A2					
Singular (das)	**Plural (die)**	**Meaning**	**Singular (das)**	**Plural (die)**	**Meaning**
Drehbuch	Drehbücher	*Script*	Sportgeschäft	Sportgeschäfte	*Sports-store*
Forum	Foren	*Forum*	Standesamt	Standesämter	*Registrar-office*
Gericht	Gerichte	*Court*	Univiertel	Univiertel	*Uni Quarter*
Mehl	Mehle	*Flour*	Zeugnis	Zeugnisse	*Transcript*

Ap.3 Fitness

Masculine Nouns from this theme for A2					
Singular (der)	**Plural (die)**	**Meaning**	**Singular (der)**	**Plural (die)**	**Meaning**
Behälter	Behälter	*Container*	Stapel	Stapel	*Pile*
Gleitschirm	Gleitschirme	*Paraglider*	Star	Stars	*(Sports)Star*
Helm	Helme	*Helmet*	Tresor	Tresore	*Vault*
Muskel	Muskeln	*Muscle*	Wahnsinn	-	*Madness*
Schatz	Schätze	*Treasure*	Wald	Wälder	*Forest*
Sieg	Siege	*Victory*	Weiderspruh	Weidersprüche	*Contradiction*
Sportler	Sportler	*Sportsman*	Yogakurs	Yogakurse	*Yoga-course*

Feminine Nouns from this theme for A2					
Singular (die)	**Plural (die)**	**Meaning**	**Singular (die)**	**Plural (die)**	**Meaning**
Begeisterung	-	*Enthusiasm*	Niederlage	Niederlagen	*Defeat*
Dose	Dosen	*Can*	Pflanze	Pflanzen	*Plant*
Enttäuschung	Enttäuschungen	*Disappointment*	Reaktion	Reaktionen	*Reaction*
Hoffnung	Hoffnungen	*Hope*	Temperatur	Temperaturen	*Temperature*
Höhle	Höhlen	*Cave*	Übersicht	Übersichten	*Overview*
Mannschaft	Mannschaften	*Team*	Unterscheidung	Unterscheidungen	*Distinction*
Natur	-	*Nature*	Yogamatte	Yogamatten	*Yoga mat*

Neutral Nouns from this theme for A2					
Singular (das)	**Plural (die)**	**Meaning**	**Singular (das)**	**Plural (die)**	**Meaning**
Gelände	Gelände	*Ground*	Spiel	Spiele	*Game*
Grad	Grade	*Degree*	Tier	Tiere	*Animal*
Kärtchen	Kärtchen	*Card*	Tor	Tore	*Goal*
Loch	Löcher	*Hole*	Versteck	Verstecke	*Hide*
Pferd	Pferde	*Horse*	Vorbild	Vorbilder	*Example*
Plastik	-	*Plastic*			

Ap.4 Being Professional

Masculine Nouns from this theme for A2					
Singular (der)	Plural (die)	Meaning	Singular (der)	Plural (die)	Meaning
Arztkittel	Arztkittel	*Apron*	Kamm	Kämme	*Comb*
Aspekt	Aspekte	*Aspect*	Overall	Overalls	*Overalls*
Austauch	-	*Exchange*	Schalter	Scahlter	*Counter*
Bahnsteig	Bahnsteige	*Platform*	Senior	Senioren	*Senior*
Berufwechsel	Berufwechsel	*Job switch*	Tiertrainer	Tiertrainer	*Pet trainer*
Friseur	Friseure	*Hair-dresser*	Tischler	Tischler	*Carpenter*
Gang	Gänge	*Gear*	Vermieter	Vermieter	*Landlord*
Hammer	Hammer	*Hammer*	Waggon	Waggons	*Wagon*

Feminine Nouns from this theme for A2					
Singular (die)	Plural (die)	Meaning	Singular (die)	Plural (die)	Meaning
Abfahrt	Abfahrten	*Departure*	Nachricht	Nachrichten	*News*
Auskunft	Auskünfte	*Info desk*	Parallele	Parallelen	*Parallel*
Dame	Damen	*Lady*	Reservierung	Reservirungen	*Reservation*
Durchwahl	Durchwahlen	*Extension*	Ruhe	-	*Quiet*
Ermäßigung	Ermäßigungen	*Discount*	Schere	Scheren	*Scissors*
Fähigkeit	Fähigkeiten	*Ability*	Tat	Taten	*Deed*
Flexibilität	-	*Flexibility*	Tönung	Tönungen	*Tint*
Hierarchie	Hierarchien	*Hierarchy*	Vernetzung	Vernetzungen	*Networking*
Medizin	-	*Medicine*			

Neutral Nouns from this theme for A2					
Singular (das)	Plural (die)	Meaning	Singular (das)	Plural (die)	Meaning
Abteil	Abteile	*Compartment*	Musikereignis	Musikereignisse	*Concert*
Gepäck	-	*Luggage*	Schlid	Schlider	*Shield*
Gleis	Gleise	*track*	Schlüsselwort	Schlüsselwörter	*Keyword*
Herzzentrum	Herzzentren	*Center*	Schmuckstück	Schmuckstücke	*Jewellery*
Lächeln	-	*Smile*	Wissen	-	*Knowledge*

Ap.5 On the go!

Masculine Nouns from this theme for A2					
Singular (der)	Plural (die)	Meaning	Singular (der)	Plural (die)	Meaning
Abflug	Abflüge	*Departure*	Fußballer	Fußballer	*Footballer*
Anbieter	Anbieter	*Provider*	Kriminelle	Kriminellen	*Criminal*
Anschluss	Anschlüsse	*Connection*	Ordner	Ordner	*Folder*
Ausgang	Ausgänge	*Exit*	Schriftsteller	Schriftsteller	*Writer*

Ausländer	Ausländer	*Foreigner*	Stau	Staus	*Traffic-jam*
Buchverlag	Buchverlage	*Publication*	Stern	Sterne	*Star*
Durchschnitt	Durchschnitte	*Average*	Verkehr	-	*Traffic*
Elefant	Elefanten	*Elephant*	Vertrag	Verträge	*Contract*
Enkel	Enkel	*Grandson*	Zuschauer	Zuschauer	*Spectator*

Feminine Nouns from this theme for A2					
Singular (die)	**Plural (die)**	**Meaning**	**Singular (die)**	**Plural (die)**	**Meaning**
Begegung	Begegungen	*Encounter*	Strecke	Strecken	*Route*
Brücke	Brücken	*Bridge*	Szene	Szenen	*Scene*
Enkelin	Enkelinen	*Granddaughter*	Tankstelle	Tankstellen	*Petrol pump*
Gebühr	Gebühren	*Fee*	Tastatur	Tastaturen	*Keyboard*
Gefahr	Gefahren	*Danger*	Überlegung	Überlegungen	*Consideration*
Isomatte	Isomatten	*Sleeping mat*	Umfrage	Umfragen	*Survey*
Kreuzung	Kreuzungen	*Crossing*	Unterwäsche	-	*Underwear*
Not	Nöte	*Need*	Versicherung	Versicherungen	*Insurance*
Panne	Pannen	*Breakdown*	Versöhnung	Versöhnungen	*Reconsiliation*
Romanze	Romanzen	*Romance*	Verteilung	Verteilungen	*Distribution*
Runde	Runden	*Round*	Wäsche	-	*Laundry*
Schlange	Schlangen	*Snake*	Werbung	Werbungen	*Advertising*
Sendung	Sendungen	*Broadcast*	Wollmütze	Wollmützen	*Woolen cap*

Neutral Nouns from this theme for A2					
Singular (das)	**Plural (die)**	**Meaning**	**Singular (das)**	**Plural (die)**	**Meaning**
Benzin	-	*Petrol*	Notizbuch	Notizbücher	*Notce-book*
Ersatzteil	Ersatzteile	*Spares*	Parkhaus	Parkhäuser	*Parking*
Fernehgerät	Fernsehgeräte	*Television*	Porträt	Porträts	*Portrait*
Kennzeichen	Kennzeichen	*Identification*	Shooting	Shootings	*Shooting*
Klischee	Klischees	*Cliché*	Stadion	Stadien	*Stadium*
Lachen	-	*Laugh*	Vorhaben	-	*Project*
Laufwerk	Laufwerke	*Drive*	Vorurteil	Vorurteile	*Prejudice*
Medium	Medien	*Medium*	Werkzeug	Werkzeuge	*Tool*
Mitglied	Mitglieder	*Member*			

Ap.6 Exploring cities and Travel

Masculine Nouns from this theme for A2					
Singular (der)	Plural (die)	Meaning	Singular (der)	Plural (die)	Meaning
Chor	Chöre	*Choir*	Kakao	Kakaos	*Cocoa*
Fernsehturm	-	*Watch tower*	Ofen	Öfen	*Oven*
Filmgesseur	Filmgesseure	*Film maker*	Promi	Promis	*Celebrity*
Gast	Gäste	*Guest*	Quatsch	-	*Crap*
Gastgeber	Gastgeber	*Host*	Rabatt	Rabatte	*Discount*
Geselle	Gesellen	*Companion*	Solist	Solisten	*Soloist*
Handkuss	Handküsse	*Hand-kiss*	Umbau	Umbauten	*Modification*

Feminine Nouns from this theme for A2					
Singular (die)	Plural (die)	Meaning	Singular (die)	Plural (die)	Meaning
Absicht	Absichten	*Intension*	Realität	-	*Reality*
Arena	Arenen	*Arena*	Rolle	Rollen	*Role*
Ecke	Ecken	*Corner*	Stille	-	*Silence*
Führung	Führungen	*Guidence*	Unterhaltung	Unterhaltungen	*Recreation*
Geschichte	Geschichten	*History*	Verfilmung	Verfilmungen	*Filming*
Kaiserzeit	-	*Imperial*	Walz	-	*Waltz*
Qualität	-	*Quality*	Wirtschaft	-	*Business*
Quittung	Quittungen	*Receipt*	Zeremonie	Zeremonien	*Ceremony*

Neutral Nouns from this theme for A2					
Singular (das)	Plural (die)	Meaning	Singular (das)	Plural (die)	Meaning
Album	Alben	*Album*	Konto	Konten	*Account*
Ballkleid	Ballkleider	*Ball-dress*	Konzerthaus	Konzerthäuse	*Theatre*
Benehmen	-	*Behaviour*	Lagerhaus	Lagerhäuser	*Warehouse*
Budget	Budgets	*Budget*	Schloss	Schlösser	*Castle*
Erntedankfest	Erntedankfeste	*Thanksgiving*	Skifahren	-	*Skiing*
Graffito	Graffiti	*Graffiti*	Stück	Stücke	*Piece*
Interesse	Interessen	*Interest*	Wildschwein	Wildschweine	*Wild Boar*
Jahrhundert	Jahrhunderte	*Century*			

Ap.7 Expressing yourself

Masculine Nouns from this theme for A2					
Singular (der)	**Plural (die)**	**Meaning**	**Singular (der)**	**Plural (die)**	**Meaning**
Absatz	Absätze	*Paragraph*	Grund	Gründe	*Reason*
Aufenthalt	Aufenthalte	*Stay*	Kiosk	Kioske	*Kiosk*
Blogeintrag	Blogeinträge	*Blog*	Kreis	Kreise	*Circle*
Blumestrauß	Blumensträuße	*Flower bunch*	Ring	Ringe	*Ring*
Gegensatz	Gegensätze	*Contrast*	Schultag	Schultage	*school-day*
Glückwunsch	Glückwünsche	*Congratulations*	Stork	Störche	*Stork*

Feminine Nouns from this theme for A2					
Singular (die)	**Plural (die)**	**Meaning**	**Singular (die)**	**Plural (die)**	**Meaning**
Absage	Absagen	*Cancellation*	Rose	Rosen	*Rose*
Achterbahn	Achterbahnen	*Rollercoaster*	Schultüte	Schultüten	*School-bag*
Angst	Ängste	*Anxiety*	Sehensucht	Sehensüchte	*Desire*
Freundschaft	Freundschaften	*Friendship*	Stimmung	-	*Mood*
Geburt	Geburten	*Birth*	Variante	Varianten	*Variant*
Geduld	-	*Patience*	Veranstaltung	Veranstaltungen	*Event*
Liebe	-	*Love*	Wunde	Wunden	*Wound*
Medaille	Medaillen	*Medal*	Zeitreise	Zeitreise	*Time-travel*
Musikstil	Musikstile	*Genre*			

Neutral Nouns from this theme for A2					
Singular (das)	**Plural (die)**	**Meaning**	**Singular (das)**	**Plural (die)**	**Meaning**
Abenteuer	Abenteuer	*Adventure*	Gras	Gräser	*Grass*
Abiturzeugnis	Abiturzeugnisse	*Diploma*	Heimweh	-	*Homesick*
Ausland	-	*Foreign*	Jubiläum	Jubiläen	*Anniversary*
Bedauern	-	*Regret*	Kajak	Kajaks	*Kayak*
Blut	-	*Blood*	Kerzenlicht	Kerzenlichter	*Candle-light*
Brautpaar	Brautpaare	*Couple*	Muss	-	*Must*
Ereignis	Ereignise	*Event*	Pech	-	*Bad luck*
Festival	Festivals	*Festival*	Sportfest	Sportfeste	*Sportfest*
Feuerwerk	Feuerwerke	*Firework*	Stadtfest	Stadtfeste	*Cityfest*
Gefühl	Gefühle	*Feeling*	Theaterfest	Theaterfeste	*Theaterfest*
Glück	-	*Luck*	Unglück	-	*Bad Luck*
Gold	-	*Gold*	Wohnheim	Wohnheime	*Dormitory*

Appendix 2. List of Regular Verbs for A2 and Conjugation Tables

Infinitiv	Präsens (er)	Präteritum (er)	Partizip II
ändern	ändert	änderte	hat geändert
äußern	äußert	äußerte	hat geäußert
backen	backt	backte	hat gebacken
balancieren	balanciert	balancierte	hat balanciert
bauen	baut	baute	hat gebaut
bedanken	bedankt	bedankte	hat bedankt
beeilen	beeilt	beeilte	hat beeilt
beeindrucken	beeindruckt	beeindruckte	hat beeindruckt
belieben	beliebt	beliebte	hat beliebt
bellen	bellt	bellte	hat gebellt
belohnen	belohnt	belohnte	hat belohnt
bereuen	bereut	bereute	hat bereut
bestehen	besteht	bestand	hat bestanden
bestimmen	bestimmt	bestimmte	hat bestimmt
betonen	betont	betonte	hat betont
betreuen	betreut	betreute	hat betreut
blicken	blickt	blickte	hat geblickt
buchen	bucht	buchte	hat gebucht
checken	checkt	checkte	hat gecheckt
decken	deckt	deckte	hat gedeckt
dekorieren	dekoriert	dekorierte	hat dekoriert
diktieren	diktiert	diktierte	hat diktiert
dolmetschen	dolmetscht	dolmetschte	hat gedolmetscht
engagieren	engagiert	engagierte	hat engagiert
entdecken	entdeckt	entdeckte	hat entdeckt
entstehen	entsteht	entstand	ist entstanden
entwerfen	entwerft	entwarf	hat entworfen
erfragen	erfragt	erfragte	hat erfragt
erfüllen	erfüllt	erfüllte	hat erfüllt
erholen	erholt	erholte	hat erholt
erlauben	erlaubt	erlaubte	hat erlaubt
erleben	erlebt	erlebte	hat erlebt
erledigen	erledigt	erledigte	hat erledigte
erreichen	erreicht	erreicht	hat erreicht
erscheinen	erscheint	erschien	ist erschienen
erwähnen	erwähnt	erwähnte	hat erwähnt
existieren	existiert	existierte	hat existiert
faszinieren	fasziniert	faszinierte	hat fasziniert
flüstern	flüstert	flüsterte	hat geflüstert

Infinitiv	Präsens (er)	Präteritum (er)	Partizip II
föhnen	föhnt	föhnte	hat geföhnt
folgen	folgt	folgte	ist gefolgt
führen	führt	führte	hat geführt
füttern	füttert	fütterte	hat gefüttert
gewöhnen	gewöhnt	gewöhnte	hat gewöhnt
handeln	handelt	handelte	hat gehandelt
heilen	heilt	heilte	ist geheilt
hoffen	hofft	hoffte	hat gehofft
interviewen	interviewt	interviewte	hat interviewt
kämmen	kämmt	kämmte	hat gekämmt
kapieren	kapiert	kapierte	hat kapiert
kleben	klebt	klebte	hat geklebt
klicken	klickt	klickte	hat geklickt
klingeln	klingelt	klingelte	hat geklingelt
kommentieren	kommentiert	kommentierte	hat kommentiert
konzentrieren	konzentriert	konzentrierte	hat konzentriert
kopieren	kopiert	kopierte	hat kopiert
korrigieren	korrigiert	korrigierte	hat korrigiert
kriegen	kriegt	kriegte	hat gekriegt
kümmern	kümmert	kümmerte	hat gekümmert
kündigen	kündigt	kündigte	hat gekündigt
lächeln	lächelt	lächelte	hat gelächelt
langweilen	langweilt	langweilte	ist gelangweilt
leeren	leert	leerte	hat geleert
lehnen	lehnt	lehnte	hat gelehnt
leihen	leiht	lieh	hat geliehen
lenken	lenkt	lenkte	hat gelenkt
lohnen	lohnt	lohnte	hat gelohnt
lügen	lügt	log	hat gelogen
mischen	mischt	mischte	hat gemischt
moderieren	moderiert	moderierte	hat moderiert
motivieren	motiviert	motivierte	hat motiviert
nerven	nervt	nervte	hat genervt
parken	parkt	parkte	hat geparkt
pendeln	pendelt	pendelte	ist gependelt
qualifizieren	qualifiziert	qualifizierte	hat qualifiziert
queren	quert	querte	hat gequert
rasieren	rasiert	rasierte	hat rasiert
regen	regt	regte	hat geregt
reiben	reibt	rieb	hat gerieben

Infinitiv	Präsens (er)	Präteritum (er)	Partizip II
reichen	reicht	reichte	hat gereicht
rennen	rennt	rannte	ist gerannt
ruhen	ruht	ruhte	hat geruht
rühren	rührt	rührte	hat gerührt
schälen	schält	schälte	hat geschält
schaukeln	schaukelt	schaukelte	ist geschaukelt
schlürfen	schlürft	schlürfte	hat geschlürft
sorgen	sorgt	sorgte	hat gesorgt
sortieren	sortiert	sortierte	hat sortiert
sparen	spart	sparte	hat gespart
speichern	speichert	speicherte	hat gespeichert
spiegeln	spiegelt	spiegelte	hat gespiegelt
springen	springt	sprang	ist gesprungen
spülen	spült	spülte	ist gespült
stecken	steckt	steckte	hat gesteckt
stinken	stinkt	stank	hat gestunken
stören	stört	störte	hat gestört
streuen	streut	streute	hat gestreut
tanken	tankt	tankte	hat getankt
teilen	teilt	teilte	hat geteilt
trennen	trennt	trennte	hat getrennet
üben	übt	übte	hat geübt
überlegen	überlegt	überlegte	hat überlegt
überqueren	überquert	überquerte	hat überquert
überreichen	überreicht	überreichte	hat überreicht
verändern	verändert	veränderte	hat verändert
verbessern	verbessert	verbesserte	hat verbessert
verbringen	verbringt	verbrachte	hat verbracht
vergehen	vergeht	verging	ist vergangen
verlieren	verliert	verlor	hat verloren
verplanen	verplant	verplante	hat verplant
verirren	verirrt	verrirte	ist verirrt
verschieben	verschiebt	verschob	hat verschoben
verstauen	verstaut	verstaute	ist verstaut
verstecken	versteckt	versteckte	hat versteckt
versuchen	versucht	versuchte	hat versucht
weinen	weint	weinte	hat geweint
wirken	wirkt	wirkte	hat gewirkt
wundern	wundert	wunderte	hat gewundert
wünschen	wünscht	wünschte	hat gewünscht

| zählen | zählt | zählte | hat gezählt |
| zerstreuen | zerstreut | zerstreute | hat zerstreut |

Following tables contain the verb conjugations of all the regular verbs listed for A2

	ändern to alter	**äußern** to express	**backen** to bake	**balancieren** to balance	**bauen** to build
ich	ändere	äußere	backe	balanciere	baue
du	änderst	äußerst	backst	balancierst	baust
er/sie/es	ändert	äußert	backt	balanciert	baut
wir	ändern	äußeren	backen	balancieren	bauen
ihr	ändert	äußert	backt	balanciert	baut
sie/Sie	ändern	äußeren	backen	balancieren	bauen

	bedanken to appreciate	**beeilen** to hurry	**beeindrucken** to impress	**belieben** to like	**bellen** to bark
ich	bedanke	beeile	beeindrucke	beliebe	belle
du	bedankst	beeilst	beeindruckst	beliebst	bellst
er/sie/es	bedankt	beeilt	beeindruckt	beliebt	bellt
wir	bedanken	beeilen	beeindrucken	belieben	bellen
ihr	bedankt	beeilt	beeindruckt	beliebt	bellt
sie/Sie	bedanken	beeilen	beeindrucken	belieben	bellen

	belohnen to reward	**bereuen** to regret	**bestehen** to pass	**bestimmen** to determine	**betonen** to emphasize
ich	belohne	bereue	bestehe	bestimme	betone
du	belohnst	bereust	bestehst	bestimmst	betonst
er/sie/es	belohnt	bereut	besteht	bestimmt	betont
wir	belohnen	bereuen	bestehen	bestimmen	betonen
ihr	belohnt	bereut	besteht	bestimmt	betont
sie/Sie	belohnen	bereuen	bestehen	bestimmen	betonen

	betreuen to look after	**blicken** to glimpse	**buchen** to book	**checken** to check	**decken** to cover	**dekorieren** to decorate
ich	betreue	blicke	buche	checke	decke	dekoriere
du	betreust	blickst	buchst	checkst	deckst	dekorierst
er/sie/es	betreut	blicht	bucht	checkt	deckt	dekoriert
wir	betreuen	blicken	buchen	checken	decken	dekorieren
ihr	betreut	blickt	bucht	checkt	deckt	dekoriert
sie/Sie	betreuen	blicken	buchen	checken	decken	dekorieren

	diktieren to dictate	**dolmetschen** to interpret	**engagieren** to get involved	**entdecken** to discover
ich	diktiere	dolmetsche	engagiere	entdecke
du	diktierst	dolmetschst	engagierst	entdeckst
er/sie/es	diktiert	dolmetscht	engagiert	entdeckt
wir	diktieren	dolmetschen	engagieren	entdecken
ihr	diktiert	dolmetscht	engagiert	entdeckt
sie/Sie	diktieren	dolmetschen	engagieren	entdecken

	entstehen to originate	**entwerfen** to design	**erfragen** to request	**erfüllen** to fulfill	**erholen** to recover
ich	entstehe	entwerfe	erfrage	erfülle	erhole
du	entstehst	entwerfst	erfragst	erfüllst	erholst
er/sie/es	entsteht	entwerft	erfragt	erfüllt	erholt
wir	entstehen	entwerfen	erfragen	erfüllen	erholen
ihr	entsteht	entwerft	erfragt	erfüllt	erholt
sie/Sie	entstehen	entwerfen	erfregen	erfüllen	erholen

	erlauben to allow	**erleben** to experience	**erledigen** to handle	**erreichen** to reach	**erscheinen** to appear
ich	erlaube	erlebe	erledige	erreiche	erscheine
du	erlaubst	erlebst	erledigst	erreichst	erscheinst
er/sie/es	erlaubt	erlebt	erledigt	erreicht	erscheint
wir	erlauben	erleben	erledigen	erreichen	erscheinen
ihr	erlaubt	erlebt	erledigt	erreicht	erscheint
sie/Sie	erlauben	erleben	erledigen	erreichen	erscheinen

	erwähnen to mention	**existieren** to exist	**faszinieren** to fascinate	**flüstern** to whisper	**föhnen** to blow-dry
ich	erwähne	existiere	fasziniere	flüstere	föhne
du	erwähnst	existierst	faszinierst	flüsterst	föhnst
er/sie/es	erwähnt	existiert	fasziniert	flüstert	föhnt
wir	erwähnen	existieren	faszinieren	flüstern	föhnen
ihr	erwähnt	existiert	fasziniert	flüstert	föhnt
sie/Sie	erwähnen	existieren	faszinieren	flüstern	föhnen

	folgen to follow	**führen** to guide	**füttern** to feed	**gewöhnen** get used to	**handeln** to be about	**heilen** to heal
ich	folge	führe	füttere	gewöhne	handele	heile
du	folgst	führst	fütterst	gewöhnst	handelst	heilst
er/sie/es	folgt	führt	füttert	gewöhnt	handelt	heilt
wir	folgen	führen	füttern	gewöhnen	handeln	heilen
ihr	folgt	führt	füttert	gewöhnt	handelt	heilt
sie/Sie	folgen	führen	füttern	gewöhnen	handeln	heilen

	hoffen to hope	**interviewen** to interview	**kämmen** to comb	**kapieren** to understand	**kleben** to stick
ich	hoffe	interviewe	kämme	kapiere	klebe
du	hoffst	interviewst	kämmst	kapierst	klebst
er/sie/es	hofft	interviewt	kämmt	kapiert	klebt
wir	hoffen	interviewen	kämmen	kapieren	kleben
ihr	hofft	interviewt	kämmt	kapiert	klebt
sie/Sie	hoffen	interviewen	kämmen	kapieren	kleben

	klicken to click	**klingeln** to ring	**kommentieren** to comment	**konzentrieren** to concentrate	**kopieren** to copy
ich	klicke	klingele	kommentiere	konzentriere	kopiere
du	klickst	klingelst	kommentierst	konzentrierst	kopierst
er/sie/es	klickt	klingelt	kommentiert	konzentriert	kopiert
wir	klicken	klingeln	kommentieren	konzentrieren	kopieren
ihr	klickt	klingelt	kommentiert	konzentriert	kopiert
sie/Sie	klicken	klingeln	kommentieren	konzentrieren	kopieren

	korrigieren to correct	**kriegen** to obtain	**kümmern** to take care of	**kündigen** to resign, quit	**lächeln** to smile
ich	korrigiere	kriege	kümmere	kündige	lächele
du	korrigierst	kriegst	kümmerst	kündigst	lächelst
er/sie/es	korrigiert	kriegt	kümmert	kündigt	lächelt
wir	korrigieren	kriegen	kümmern	kündigen	lächeln
ihr	korrigiert	kriegt	kümmert	kündigt	lächelt
sie/Sie	korrigieren	kriegen	kümmern	kündigen	lächeln

	langweilen to bore	**leeren** to empty	**lehnen** to lean	**leihen** to borrow	**lenken** to steer	**lohnen** to be worth
ich	langweile	leere	lehne	leihe	lenke	lohne
du	langweilst	leerst	lehnst	leihst	lenkst	lohnst
er/sie/es	langweilt	leert	lehnt	leiht	lenkt	lohnt
wir	langweilen	leeren	lehnen	leihen	lenken	lohnen
ihr	langweilt	leert	lehnt	leiht	lenkt	lohnt
sie/Sie	langweilen	leeren	lehnen	leihen	lenken	lohnen

	lügen to lie	**mischen** to mix	**moderieren** to moderate	**motivieren** to motivate	**nerven** to annoy	**parken** to park
ich	lüge	mische	moderiere	motiviere	nerve	parke
du	lügst	mischst	moderierst	motivierst	nervst	parkst
er/sie/es	lügt	mischt	moderiert	motiviert	nervt	parkt
wir	lügen	mischen	moderieren	motivieren	nerven	parken
ihr	lügt	mischt	moderiert	motiviert	nervt	parkt
sie/Sie	lügen	mischen	moderieren	motivieren	nerven	parken

	pendeln to commute	**qualifizieren** to qualify	**queren** to traverse	**rasieren** to shave	**regen** to stimulate
ich	pendele	qualifiziere	quere	rasiere	rege
du	pendelst	qualifizierst	querst	rasierst	regst
er/sie/es	pendelt	qualifiziert	quert	rasiert	regt
wir	pendeln	qualifizieren	queren	rasieren	regen
ihr	pendelt	qualifiziert	quert	rasiert	regt
sie/Sie	pendeln	qualifizieren	queren	rasieren	regen

	reiben to rub	**reichen** to submit	**rennen** to rush to	**ruhen** to rest	**rühren** to stir	**schälen** to peel
ich	reibe	reiche	renne	ruhe	rühre	schäle
du	reibst	reichst	rennst	ruhst	rührst	schälst
er/sie/es	reibt	reicht	rennt	ruht	rührt	schält
wir	reiben	reichen	rennen	ruhen	rühren	schälen
ihr	reibt	reicht	rennt	ruht	rührt	schält
sie/Sie	reiben	reichen	rennen	ruhen	rühren	schälen

	schaukeln to rock/sway	schlürfen to slurp	sorgen to ensure	sortieren to sort	sparen to spare, save
ich	schaukele	schlürfe	sorge	sortiere	spare
du	schaukelst	schlürfst	sorgst	sortierst	sparst
er/sie/es	schaukelt	schlürft	sorgt	sortiert	spart
wir	schaukeln	schlürfen	sorgen	sortieren	sparen
ihr	schaukelt	schlürft	sorgt	sortiert	spart
sie/Sie	schaukeln	schlürfen	sorgen	sortieren	sparen

	speichern to save/retain	spiegeln to reflect	springen to jump	spülen to rinse	stecken to be stuck
ich	speichere	spiegele	springe	spüle	stecke
du	speicherst	spiegelst	springst	spülst	steckst
er/sie/es	speichert	spiegelt	springt	spült	steckt
wir	speichern	spiegeln	springen	spülen	stecken
ihr	speichert	spiegelt	springt	spült	steckt
sie/Sie	speichern	spiegeln	springen	spülen	stecken

	stinken to stink	stören to disturb	streuen to sprinkle	tanken to refuel	teilen to share
ich	stinke	störe	streue	tanke	teile
du	stinkst	störst	streust	tankst	teilst
er/sie/es	stinkt	stört	streut	tankt	teilt
wir	stinken	stören	streuen	tanken	teilen
ihr	stinkt	stört	streut	tankt	teilt
sie/Sie	stinken	stören	streuen	tanken	teilen

	trennen to separate	üben to practise	überlegen to think about	überqueren to cross	überreichen to hand over
ich	trenne	übe	überlege	überquere	überreiche
du	trennst	übst	überlegst	überquerst	überreichst
er/sie/es	trennt	übt	überlegt	überquert	überreicht
wir	trennen	üben	überlegen	überqueren	überreichen
ihr	trennt	übt	überlegt	überquert	überreicht
sie/Sie	trennen	üben	überlegen	überqueren	überreichen

	verändern to alter	**verbessern** to improve	**verbringen** to spend time	**vergehen** to go by (time)	**verlieren** to lose
ich	veränder	verbessere	verbringe	vergehe	verliere
du	veränderst	verbesserst	verbringst	vergehst	verlierst
er/sie/es	verändert	verbessert	verbringt	vergeht	verliert
wir	veränderen	verbessern	verbringen	vergehen	verlieren
ihr	verändert	verbessert	verbringt	vergeht	verliert
sie/Sie	veränderen	verbessern	verbringen	vergehen	verlieren

	verplanen to schedule	**verirren** to get lost	**verschieben** to delay	**verstauen** to stow	**verstecken** to hide
ich	verplane	verirre	verschiebe	verstaue	verstecke
du	verplanst	verirrst	verschiebst	verstaust	versteckst
er/sie/es	verplant	verirrt	verschiebt	verstaut	versteckt
wir	verplanen	verirren	verschieben	verstauen	verstecken
ihr	verplant	verirrt	verschiebt	verstaut	versteckt
sie/Sie	verplanen	verirren	verschieben	verstauen	verstecken

	versuchen to attempt	**weinen** to cry	**wirken** to seem	**wundern** be surprised	**wünschen** to wish
ich	versuche	weine	wirke	wundere	wünsche
du	versuchst	weinst	wirkst	wunderst	wünschst
er/sie/es	versucht	weint	wirkt	wundert	wünscht
wir	versuchen	weinen	wirken	wundern	wünschen
ihr	versucht	weint	wirkt	wundert	wünscht
sie/Sie	versuchen	weinen	wirken	wundern	wünschen

	zählen to count	**zerstreuen** to scatter
ich	zähle	zerstreue
du	zählst	zerstreust
er/sie/es	zählt	zerstreut
wir	zählen	zerstreuen
ihr	zählt	zerstreut
sie/Sie	zählen	zerstreuen

Appendix 3. List of Irregular Verbs for A2 and Conjugation Tables

Infinitiv	Präsens (er)	Präteritum (er)	Partizip II
befürchten	befürchtet	befürchtete	hat befürchtet
begleiten	begleitet	begleitete	hat begleitet
begraben	begräbt	begrub	hat begraben
begründen	begründet	begründete	hat begründet
begrüßen	begrüßt	begrüßte	hat begrüßt
benehmen	benimmt	benahm	hat benommen
besitzen	besitzt	besaß	hat besessen
bluten	blutet	blutete	hat geblutet
bremsen	bremst	bremste	hat gebremst
deuten	deutet	deutete	hat gedeutet
entnehmen	entnimmt	entnahm	hat entnommen
erfinden	erfindet	erfand	hat erfunden
erhalten	erhält	erhielt	hat erhalten
erschließen	erschließt	erschloss	hat erschlossen
erwachsen	erwächst	erwuchs	ist erwachsen
erwarten	erwartet	erwartete	hat erwartet
fassen	fasst	fasste	hat gefasst
faxen	faxt	faxte	hat gefaxt
fließen	fließt	floss	ist geflossen
gebären	gabiert	gebar	hat geboren
gelten	gilt	galt	hat gegolten
gestalten	gestaltet	gestaltete	hat gestaltet
gießen	gießt	goss	hat gegossen
gründen	gründet	gründete	hat gegründet
heiraten	heiratet	heiratete	hat geheiratet
landen	landet	landete	ist gelandet
mieten	mietet	mietete	hat gemietet
pflanzen	pflanzt	pflanzte	hat gepflanzt
posten	postet	postete	hat gepostet
rechnen	rechnet	rechnete	hat gerechnet
reiten	reitet	ritt	ist geritten
richten	richtet	richtete	hat gerichtet
rösten	röstet	röstete	hat geröstet
schießen	schießt	schoss	ist geschossen
schützen	schützt	schützte	hat geschützt
simsen	simst	simste	hat gesimst
sterben	stirbt	starb	ist gestorben
streiten	streitet	stritt	hat gestritten
töten	tötet	tötete	hat getötet

Infinitiv	Präsens (er)	Präteritum (er)	Partizip II
unterhalten	unterhaltet	unterhielt	hat unterhalten
überweisen	überweist	überwies	hat überwiesen
verbieten	verbietet	verbot	hat verboten
verfassen	verfasst	verfasste	hat verfasst
verlaufen	verläuft	verlief	ist verlaufen
vermieten	vermietet	vermietete	hat vermietet
vermuten	vermutet	vermutete	hat vermutet
verschlafen	verschläft	verschlief	hat verschlafen
verschwinden	verschwindet	verschwand	ist verschwunden
versprechen	verspricht	versprach	hat versprochen
vertreten	vertritt	vertrat	ist vertreten
wachsen	wächst	wuchs	ist gewachsen
weisen	weist	wies	hat gewiesen
werben	wirbt	warb	hat geworben
werfen	wirfst	warf	hat geworfen

Following tables contain the verb conjugations of all the irregular verbs listed for A2

	befürchten to fear	begleiten to accompany	begraben to bury	begründen to justify	begrüßen to greet
ich	befürchte	begleite	begrabe	begründe	begrüße
du	befürchtest	begleitest	begräbst	begründest	begrüßt
er/sie/es	befürchtet	begleitet	begräbt	begründet	begrüßt
wir	befürchten	begleiten	begraben	begründen	begrüßen
ihr	befürchtet	begleitet	begrabt	begründet	begrüßt
sie/Sie	befürchten	begleiten	begraben	begründen	begrüßen

	benehmen to behave	besitzen to own	bluten to bleed	bremsen to brake	deuten to indicate	entnehmen to remove
ich	benehme	besitze	blute	bremse	deute	entnehme
du	benimmst	besitzt	blutest	bremst	deutest	entnimmst
er/sie/es	benimmt	besitzt	blutet	bremst	deutet	entnimmt
wir	benehmen	besitzen	bluten	bremsen	deuten	entnehmen
ihr	benehmt	besitzt	blutet	bremst	deutet	entnehmt
sie/Sie	benehmen	besitzen	bluten	bremsen	deuten	entnehmen

	erfinden to invent	**erhalten** to receive	**erschließen** to infer	**erwachsen** to grow	**erwarten** to await
ich	erfinde	erhalte	erschließe	erwachse	erwarte
du	erfindest	erhältst	erschließt	erwächst	erwartest
er/sie/es	erfindet	erhält	erschließt	erwächst	erwartet
wir	erfinden	erhalten	erschließen	erwachsen	erwarten
ihr	erfindet	erhaltet	erschließt	erwachst	erwartet
sie/Sie	erfinden	erhalten	erschließen	erwachsen	erwarten

	fassen to grasp	**faxen** to fax	**fließen** to flow	**gebären** give birth	**gelten** to apply, count	**gestalten** to shape
ich	fasse	faxe	fließe	gebäre	gelte	gestalte
du	fasst	faxt	fließt	gabierst	giltst	gestaltest
er/sie/es	fasst	faxt	fließt	gabiert	gilt	gestaltet
wir	fassen	faxen	fließen	gebären	gelten	gestalten
ihr	fasst	faxt	fließt	gebärt	geltet	gestaltet
sie/Sie	fassen	faxen	fließen	gebärn	gelten	gestalten

	gießen to pour	**gründen** to establish	**heiraten** to marry	**landen** to land	**mieten** to rent	**pflanzen** to plant
ich	gieße	gründe	heirate	lande	miete	pflanze
du	gießt	gründest	heiratest	landest	mietest	pflanzt
er/sie/es	gießt	gründet	heiratet	landet	mietet	pflanzt
wir	gießen	gründen	heiraten	landen	mieten	pflanzen
ihr	gießt	gründet	heiratet	landet	mietet	pflanzt
sie/Sie	gießen	gründen	heiraten	landen	mieten	pflanzen

	posten to post	**rechnen** to compute	**reiten** to ride	**richten** to judge	**rösten** to roast	**schießen** to shoot
ich	poste	rechne	reite	richte	röste	schieße
du	postest	rechnest	reitest	richtest	röstest	schießt
er/sie/es	postet	rechnet	reitet	richtet	röstet	schießt
wir	posten	rechnen	reiten	richten	rösten	schießen
ihr	postet	rechnet	reitet	richtet	röstet	schießt
sie/Sie	posten	rechnen	reiten	richten	rösten	schießen

	schützen to protect	simsen to text	sterben to die	streiten to argue	töten to kill	unterhalten to chat
ich	schütze	simse	sterbe	streite	töte	unterhalte
du	schützt	simst	stirbst	streitest	tötest	unterhaltest
er/sie/es	schützt	simst	stirbt	streitet	tötet	unterhaltet
wir	schützen	simsen	sterben	streiten	töten	unterhalten
ihr	schützt	simst	sterbt	streitet	tötet	unterhaltet
sie/Sie	schützen	simsen	sterben	streiten	töten	unterhalten

	überweisen to transfer	verbieten to prohibit	verfassen to write up	verlaufen to proceed	vermieten to rent
ich	überweise	verbiete	verfasse	verlaufe	vermiete
du	überweist	verbietest	verfasst	verläufst	vermietest
er/sie/es	überweist	verbietet	verfasst	verläuft	vermietet
wir	überweisen	verbieten	verfassen	verlaufen	vermieten
ihr	überweist	verbietet	verfasst	verlauft	vermietet
sie/Sie	überweisen	verbieten	verfassen	verlaufen	vermieten

	vermuten to guess	verschlafen to oversleep	verschwinden to disappear	versprechen to promise
ich	vermute	verschlafe	verschwinde	verspreche
du	vermutest	verschläfst	verschwindest	versprichst
er/sie/es	vermutet	verschläft	verschwindet	verspricht
wir	vermuten	verschlafen	verschwinden	versprechen
ihr	vermutet	verschlaft	verschwindet	versprecht
sie/Sie	vermuten	verschlafen	verschwinden	versprechen

	vertreten to represent	wachsen to grow	weisen to assign	werben to advertise	werfen to throw
ich	vertrete	wachse	weise	werbe	werfe
du	vertrittst	wächst	weist	wirbst	wirfst
er/sie/es	vertritt	wächst	weist	wirbt	wirft
wir	vertreten	wachsen	weisen	werben	werfen
ihr	vertretet	wacht	weist	werbt	werft
sie/Sie	vertreten	wachsen	weisen	werben	werfen

Appendix 4. List of Separable Verbs for A2

Basic Verb	Meaning	Separable Verb	Meaning
bauen	*to build*	aufbauen	*to establish*
bauen	*to build*	einbauen	*to incorporate*
bieten	*to offer*	anbieten	*to offer*
denken	*to think*	nachdenken	*to ponder*
drehen	*to turn*	umdrehen	*to turn around*
essen	*to eat*	aufessen	*to eat up*
fahren	*to drive*	abfahren	*to drive away*
fahren	*to drive*	hinfahren	*to drive to*
fahren	*to drive*	wegfahren	*to drive away*
fallen	*to fall*	auffallen	*to stand out*
fallen	*to fall*	einfallen	*to think of*
fassen	*to grasp*	zusammenfassen	*to summarize*
finden	*to find*	stattfinden	*to take place*
fliegen	*to fly*	abfliegen	*to depart*
fragen	*to question*	nachfragen	*to ask again*
fühlen	*to feel*	wohlfühlen	*to feel well*
geben	*to give*	abgeben	*to leave/give up*
geben	*to give*	ausgeben	*to spend/output*
geben	*to give*	eingeben	*to input*
geben	*to give*	rübergeben	*to pass over*
geben	*to give*	weitergeben	*to pass on*
geben	*to give*	wiedergeben	*to reproduce*
gehen	*to go*	durcheinandergehen	*to getmixed up*
gehen	*to go*	eingehen	*to focus on*
gehen	*to go*	entlanggehen	*to go along*
gehen	*to go*	glattgehen	*to go smoothly*
gehen	*to go*	herumgehen	*to go around*
gehen	*to go*	kaputtgehen	*to fall apart*
gehen	*to go*	losgehen	*to start*
gehen	*to go*	vorbeigehen	*to pass by*
gehen	*to go*	vorgehen	*to have precedence*
gehen	*to go*	weitergehen	*to go further*
gehören	*to belong*	dazugehören	*to fit in*
gehören	*to belong*	zusammengehören	*to fit together*
haben	*to have*	freihaben	*to be free*
haben	*to have*	vorhaben	*to have planned*
haben	*to have*	zuhaben	*to be closed*
halten	*to hold*	einhalten	*to follow/observe*
hängen	*to hang*	abhängen	*to depend*

Basic Verb	Meaning	Separable Verb	Meaning
helfen	*to help*	weiterhelfen	*to assist*
holen	*to fetch*	wiederholen	*to revise*
kennen	*to know*	auskennen	*to be familiar with*
kleben	*to stick*	zukleben	*to seal*
klicken	*to click*	anklicken	*to click*
kochen	*to cook*	einkochen	*to boil down*
kommen	*to come*	vorkommen	*to occur/happen*
kommen	*to come*	zurechtkommen	*to cope up*
kommen	*to come*	zurückkommen	*to return*
laden	*to load*	hochladen	*to upload*
laden	*to load*	runterladen	*to download*
lassen	*to let*	anlassen	*to leave on*
lassen	*to let*	hinterlassen	*to leave behind*
legen	*to set/put/place*	hineinlegen	*to insert*
legen	*to set/put/place*	überlegen	*to think over*
lehnen	*to lean*	ablehnen	*to decline*
leihen	*to borrow*	ausleihen	*to lend*
lenken	*to steer*	ablenken	*to distract*
lenken	*to steer*	einlenken	*to back down*
lesen	*to read*	ablesen	*to read off*
lesen	*to read*	mitlesen	*to read along*
lesen	*to read*	vorlesen	*to read aloud*
lösen	*to solve*	einlösen	*to encash*
machen	*to do/make*	aufmachen	*to open*
machen	*to do/make*	gutmachen	*to do well*
machen	*to do/make*	weitermachen	*to continue*
machen	*to do/make*	zumachen	*to close*
malen	*to paint*	abmalen	*to trace*
nehmen	*to take*	abnehmen	*to remove*
nehmen	*to take*	annehmen	*to accept*
nehmen	*to take*	herausnehmen	*to take out*
nehmen	*to take*	mitnehmen	*to take along*
nehmen	*to take*	teilnehmen	*to participate*
nehmen	*to take*	unternehmen	*to undertake*
nehmen	*to take*	zunehmen	*to increase*
passen	*to fit*	aufpassen	*to watch out*
räumen	*to vacate*	ausräumen	*to empty out*
regen	*to stimulate*	aufregen	*to get upset*
reiben	*to rub*	einreiben	*to rub in*
richten	*to judge*	ausrichten	*to leave a message*

Basic Verb	Meaning	Separable Verb	Meaning
rufen	*to call*	zurückrufen	*to call back*
ruhen	*to rest*	ausruhen	*to relax*
rühren	*to stir*	umrühren	*to agitate*
schalten	*to switch over to*	ausschalten	*to turn off*
schalten	*to switch over to*	einschalten	*to turn on*
schauen	*to watch*	hineinschauen	*to look into*
schlagen	*to beat*	aufschlagen	*to open*
schließen	*to close*	abschließen	*to conclude*
schreiben	*to write*	weiterschreiben	*to continue writing*
sehen	*to see*	aussehen	*to appear*
sehen	*to see*	fernsehen	*to see TV*
setzen	*to put*	fortsetzen	*to continue*
setzen	*to put*	hinsetzen	*to sit down*
spielen	*to play*	vorspielen	*to act out*
sprechen	*to speak*	aussprechen	*to pronounce*
steigen	*to climb*	aufsteigen	*to climb steps*
steigen	*to climb*	einsteigen	*to climb in*
stellen	*to put*	abstellen	*to park*
stellen	*to put*	aufstellen	*to set up*
stellen	*to put*	feststellen	*to determine*
stimmen	*to be right*	zustimmen	*to agree*
suchen	*to search*	aussuchen	*to select*
tauschen	*to exchange*	austauschen	*to trade*
teilen	*to share*	austeilen	*to distribute*
tragen	*to carry*	vortragen	*to recite/deliver*
verkaufen	*to sell*	ausverkaufen	*to sell-out*
wechseln	*to change*	abwechseln	*to alternate*
zeichnen	*to draw*	einzeichnen	*to sketch*
ziehen	*to pull*	aufziehen	*to raise*
ziehen	*to pull*	ausziehen	*to take off shoes*
ziehen	*to pull*	einziehen	*to move in*

Appendix 5. Sample sentences with Regular verbs and concepts learnt for A2 level

Verb	Meaning	Sample Sentence
ändern	*to alter*	Nach der Prüfung dürfen Sie nicht Ihre Lösungen ändern.
äußern	*to express*	Ich äußere immer meine Gefühle.
backen	*to bake*	Gestern habe ich einen Kuchen gebacken.
balancieren	*to balance*	Ich kann das Fahrrad balancieren, deshalb bin ich sehr glücklich.
bauen	*to build*	Ich lasse ein Haus bauen, deshalb finde ich keine Zeit für andere Tätigkeiten.
bedanken	*to appreciate*	Ich möchte Ihnen für diese Arbeit bedanken.
beeilen	*to hurry*	Wir müssen uns beeilen, weil wir spät sind.
beeindrucken	*to impress*	Dein höfliches Verhalten hat mich beeindruckt.
belieben	*to like*	Ich beliebe meine Eltern.
bellen	*to bark*	Ich habe nicht geschlafen, weil ein Hund hat die ganz Nacht gebellt.
belohnen	*to reward*	Ich habe ihm belohnen, denn er hat gut gearbeitet.
bereuen	*to regret*	Worüber bereust du?
bestehen	*to pass*	Ich freue mich, wenn ich eine Prüfung bestehe.
bestimmen	*to determine*	Könnten Sie Dauern für das Experiment bestimmen?
betonen	*to emphasize*	Sie muss in ihrer Aussprache wichtige Wörter betonen.
betreuen	*to look after*	Bitte betreuen Sie meinen Hund.
blicken	*to glimpse*	Du solltest blicken, dass wie Lord Venkateshwara gestern sieht.
buchen	*to book*	Ich habe Tickets für das Konzert gebuchkt.
checken	*to check*	Ich möchte Sie checken.
decken	*to cover*	Das hatte ich nicht gedacht.
dekorieren	*to decorate*	Wir dekorieren unsere Wohnung in Diwali.
diktieren	*to dictate*	Bitte schreiben Sie, was ich diktiere.
dolmetschen	*to interpret*	Kannst du mir helfen, denn ich brauche jemand einer Fremdsprache dolmetschen zu können.
engagieren	*to get involved*	Ich freue mich auf dem Konzert, deshalb engagiere ich genau mit der Mannschaft.
entdecken	*to discover*	Ich habe eine wunderbare Sache entdeckt, trotzdem will ich nicht darüber sprechen.
entstehen	*to originate*	Was für ein Thema hat, gestern entsteht?
entwerfen	*to design*	Ich kann viele Produkte entwerfen.
erfragen	*to request*	Der Mann hat erfragt, ob sie einen Kuchen essen möchte.

Verb	Meaning	Sample Sentence
erfüllen	*to fulfill*	Bitte erfüllen Sie meine Wünsche.
erholen	*to recover*	Hast du dein Geld erholt?
erlauben	*to allow*	Wir danken Ihnen, weil Sie uns dort gehen erlaubt hatten.
erleben	*to experience*	Was kann ich dort erleben?
erledigen	*to handle*	Bitte erledigen Sie sich sicherlich.
erreichen	*to reach*	Mein Vater will wissen, wann ich zu Hyderabad erreiche.
erscheinen	*to appear*	Welcher Gott hat, dort erscheint?
erwähnen	*to mention*	Sie müssen nicht Ihre privaten Informationen erwähnen.
existieren	*to exist*	Dieses Haus ist seit 100 Jahren existiert.
faszinieren	*to fascinate*	Deine höflichen Glückwünsche hat mich fasziniert.
flüstern	*to whisper*	Sie dürfen nicht flüstern, weil Sie laut und deutlich sprechen müssen.
föhnen	*to blow-dry*	Kannst du bitte den Haaren föhnen?
folgen	*to follow*	Beispiele folgt immer nach ein Konzept.
führen	*to guide*	Kann jemand ein Gespräch führen?
füttern	*to feed*	Könnten Sie meinen Hund füttern, wenn ich nicht in Hause bin?
gewöhnen	*get used to*	In ein paar Tage werden Sie gewöhnen.
handeln	*to be about*	Die Präsentation handelt über einem wichtigen Fach.
heilen	*to heal*	Er hatte einen Unfall, trotzdem heilt er in seinem Hause.
hoffen	*to hope*	Ich habe gut gehofft, deshalb geht alles gut.
interviewen	*to interview*	Er hat mich interviewt.
kämmen	*to comb*	Ich kämme mir die Haare, weil ich sauber sein möchte.
kapieren	*to understand*	Kapieren Sie, was ich sagen will?
kleben	*to stick*	Ich habe mein Foto schon geklebt.
klicken	*to click*	Ich glaube, dass wie er Fotos klicken kann.
klingeln	*to ring*	Ich bin glücklich, wenn die Klingel klingelt.
kommentieren	*to comment*	Musstest du kommentieren?
konzentrieren	*to concentrate*	Ich kann mich nicht konzentrieren.
kopieren	*to copy*	Sie dürfen nicht die Information kopieren, weil Sie selbst denken sollen.
korrigieren	*to correct*	Wir sind schon fertig und nun können Sie ihre Fehler korrigieren.
kriegen	*to obtain*	Kriegst du die Dokumente?
kümmern	*to take care of*	Bitte kümmern Sie meine Katze.
kündigen	*to resign, quit*	Als er eine schlechte Erfahrung hat, möchte er kündigen.

Verb	Meaning	Sample Sentence
lächeln	*to smile*	Warum lächelst du?
langweilen	*to bore*	Der Professor hat viel geredet und mich gelangweilt.
leeren	*to empty*	Bitte leeren Sie Ihre Flasche genau.
lehnen	*to lean*	Bitte lehnen Sie nicht an der Wand.
leihen	*to borrow*	Ich möchte für eine Woche deine Bücher leihen.
lenken	*to steer*	Ich liebe mit meinem Vater unser Auto lenken, als ich ein Kind war.
lohnen	*to be worth*	Der Urlaub lohnt mehrerr als das Geld, das wir bezahlt haben.
lügen	*to lie*	Er wusste, dass ich in der Polizei bin, trotzdem lügt er schon.
mischen	*to mix*	Ich habe Wasser und Apfelsaft gemischt.
moderieren	*to moderate*	Niemand hat die Firma moderiert, trotzdem geht alle gut.
motivieren	*to motivate*	Du hast mich gern motiviert.
nerven	*to annoy*	Die Verspätung nervt mich.
parken	*to park*	Der Mann will wissen, ob er sein Auto hier parken kann.
pendeln	*to commute*	Meistens pendele ich mit dem Bus.
qualifizieren	*to qualify*	Leider haben Sie nicht qualifiziert.
queren	*to traverse*	Wo quert das Flugzeug?
rasieren	*to shave*	Man kann rasieren, wann er so fühlt.
regen	*to stimulate*	Können Sie die Eier regnen?
reiben	*to rub*	Wenn Sie Ihre Hände reiben, fühlen Sie warme.
reichen	*to submit*	Bitte reichen Sie die Assignment morgen.
rennen	*to rush to*	Ich muss zu der Firma rennen, weil ich eine Verspätung gemacht habe.
ruhen	*to rest*	Nach der Prüfung musst du gut ruhen, weil du müde wirst.
rühren	*to stir*	Bitte rühren Sie den Kaffee zuerst und dann genießen Sie ihn.
schälen	*to peel*	Sie müssen nicht alle Kartoffeln schälen.
schaukeln	*to rock/sway*	Die Schiffe schaukelt, deshalb mache ich vielen Spaß.
schlürfen	*to slurp*	Sie dürfen die Suppe schlürfen.
sorgen	*to ensure*	Bitte sorgen Sie, dass Sie alle Dinge mitnehmen haben.
sortieren	*to sort*	Bitte sortieren Sie alle Gemüse.
sparen	*to spare, save*	Ich spare Geld, weil ich nicht ausgeben möchte.
speichern	*to save/retain*	Bitte speichern Sie genau die wichtigen Informationen.

Verb	Meaning	Sample Sentence
spiegeln	*to reflect*	Das Wasser spiegelt ein gutes Bild an der Wand.
springen	*to jump*	Herr Bean springt manchmal im Bett.
spülen	*to rinse*	Haben Sie diese Gemüse gespült?
stecken	*to be stuck*	Manchmal strecke ich in lustige Situationen.
stinken	*to stink*	Warum stinkt es hier?
stören	*to disturb*	Ich hatte ihm geärgert, weil er mich gestört hat.
streuen	*to sprinkle*	Er sollte ein bisschen Salz über dem Brot streuen.
tanken	*to refuel*	Mindestens zweimal monatlich muss ich mein Motorrad tanken.
teilen	*to share*	Kann ich das Essen mit dir teilen?
trennen	*to separate*	Bitte trennen Sie die Kartoffeln von dem anderen Gemüse.
üben	*to practise*	Wir müssen täglich Deutsch üben.
überlegen	*to think about*	Ich überlege, dass wie ich besser Aussprache sprechen kann.
überqueren	*to cross*	Bitte überqueren Sie die Straußke.
überreichen	*to hand over*	Ich habe meinem Pass die Polizei überreicht.
verändern	*to alter*	Sie dürfen nicht etwas verändern.
verbessern	*to improve*	Ihre Noten haben als letztes Jahr verbessert.
verbringen	*to spend time*	Kannst du mit mir heute Abend Zeit verbringen?
vergehen	*to go by (time)*	Es ist wunderbar, wie die Zeit vergeht!
verirren	*to get lost*	Letztes Jahr bin ich sich in Dharwad verirren.
verlieren	*to lose*	Ich hatte meine Tasche verlieren.
verplanen	*to schedule*	Der Termin verplant sich am 10.12. um 11:00 Uhr.
verschieben	*to delay*	Das habe ich schon gedacht, dass du immer das Projekt verschiebt.
verstauen	*to stow*	Ich verstaue die Flasche von Bier, weil ich Bier nicht trinke und möchte die jemand schenken.
verstecken	*to hide*	Was hast du in deinem Haus versteckt?
versuchen	*to attempt*	Ich habe meine Brille verlieren, trotzdem versuche ich, ohne Brille zu sehen.
weinen	*to cry*	Ich dachte, dass warum er weint.
wirken	*to seem*	Das wirkt mir interessant!
wundern	*be surprised*	Die Überraschung hat mich gewundert.
wünschen	*to wish*	Ich glaube, dass was er gewusst hat.
zählen	*to count*	Kannst du die Zahlen zählen?
zerstreuen	*to scatter*	Bitte zerstreuen Sie nicht etwas.

Appendix 6. Sample sentences with Irregular verbs and concepts learnt for A2 level

Verb	Meaning	Sample Sentence
befürchten	*to fear*	Er befürchtet sich, wenn er eine Prüfung schreiben muss.
begleiten	*to accompany*	Kannst du mich zum Konzert begleiten?
begraben	*to bury*	Was hast du dort begrabt?
begründen	*to justify*	Kannst du dich für den Fehler begründen?
begrüßen	*to greet*	Morgens müssen wir ein anderes begrüßen.
benehmen	*to behave*	Bitte benehmen Sie höflich.
besitzen	*to own*	Er besitzt eine Firma.
bluten	*to bleed*	Er hatte einen Unfall, deshalb blutet er.
bremsen	*to brake*	Bitte bremsen Sie Ihrem Auto ganz langsam.
deuten	*to indicate*	Anil hat einen Dokument gemacht, die alle Regeln gedeutet hat.
entnehmen	*to remove*	Bitte entnehmen Sie Ihre Schuhe.
erfinden	*to invent*	Thomas Edison erfand die Glühbirne.
erhalten	*to receive*	Ich hatte ein Geschenk erhalten.
erschließen	*to infer*	Was kann man nach dem Lesen des Kapitals erschließen?
erwachsen	*to grow*	Wir sind zusammen erwachsen.
erwarten	*to await*	Ich erwarte auf das Ergebnis.
fassen	*to grasp*	Bitte fassen Sie etwas, weil der Weg gefährlich ist.
faxen	*to fax*	Könntest du die Dokumente mich faxen?
fließen	*to flow*	Der Fluss fließt durch die Stadt.
gebären	*give birth*	Meine Freundin hat eine Tochter geboren.
gelten	*to apply, count*	Was giltst du auf den Kopf?
gestalten	*to shape*	Kann jemand mir sagen, wie man das gestaltet?
gießen	*to pour*	Gießen Sie den Wein sehr sicherlich, weil sie teuer ist.
gründen	*to establish*	Sie müssen sich gründen und machen keine Sorge.
heiraten	*to marry*	Ich möchte meine Freundin heiraten.
landen	*to land*	Unser Flugzeug hat um 20:00 Uhr gelandet.
mieten	*to rent*	Er hat seine Wohnung gemietet.
pflanzen	*to plant*	Wir müssen pro Jahr mindestens eine Pflanze pflanzen.
posten	*to post*	Hast du die Fotos gepostet?
rechnen	*to compute*	Können Sie genau mündlich rechnen?
reiten	*to ride*	Ich kann einen Pferd nicht reiten, trotzdem habe ich 10 Jahre hin in Kashmir ihn geritten.

Verb	Meaning	Sample Sentence
richten	*to judge*	Er mag nicht, andere Leute zu richten.
rösten	*to roast*	Ich mag Hähnchen rösten.
schießen	*to shoot*	Wo hast du den Film geschießen?
schützen	*to protect*	Wir müssen die Umwelt immer schützen.
simsen	*to text*	Simsen Sie mich von Hause.
sterben	*to die*	Der Hund ist gestorben.
streiten	*to argue*	Ich will dich nicht streiten, deshalb bin ich ruhig.
töten	*to kill*	Letztes Jahr hat meinem Freund zwei Schlangen getötet, weil sie giftlich waren.
überweisen	*to transfer*	Ich überweise das Geld sofort.
unterhalten	*to chat*	Im Unterricht müssen Sie nur auf Deutsch unterhalten.
verbieten	*to prohibit*	Ich habe Rauschen verboten.
verfassen	*to write up*	Ich möchte Ihnen sofort verfassen.
verlaufen	*to proceed*	Können wir mit dem Plan verlaufen?
vermieten	*to rent*	Hast du deine Wohnung vermietet?
vermuten	*to guess*	Können Sie die richtige Antwort vermuten?
verschlafen	*to oversleep*	Gourav ist der Mann, der nicht verschlafen hat.
verschwinden	*to disappear*	Dieser Moment war er hier und jetzt ist er verschwinden.
versprechen	*to promise*	Was möchtest du mir heute versprechen?
vertreten	*to represent*	In dem Olympia vertritt er sein Land.
wachsen	*to grow*	Er ist schnell gewacht.
weisen	*to assign*	Ich weise dir diese Tätigkeit.
werben	*to advertise*	Wir werben unsere Produkte.
werfen	*to throw*	Ich will den Müll werfen.

Appendix 7. Sample sentences with Separable verbs and concepts learnt for A2 level

Verb	Meaning	Sample Sentence
abfahren	*to drive away*	Morgen am Nachmittag fährt er nach Pune ab.
abfliegen	*to depart*	Das Flugzeug fliegt um 15:00 Uhr ab.
abgeben	*to leave/give up*	Gibst du Rauschen ab?
abhängen	*to depend*	Er hängt bei seinem Vater ab.
ablehnen	*to decline*	Möchten Sie die Angebote ablehnen?
ablenken	*to distract*	Er hat mich abgelenkt, trotzdem war ich sicherlich.
ablesen	*to read off*	Hast du den Roman in einer Nacht gelesen?
abmalen	*to trace*	Wer kann das Bild gut abmalen?
abnehmen	*to remove*	Er hat ihn abgenommen.
abschließen	*to conclude*	Ich schließe meine Präsentation in zehn Minuten ab.
abstellen	*to park*	Wo kann ich mein Auto abstellen?
abwechseln	*to alternate*	Wann müss ich die Bücher abwechseln?
anbieten	*to offer*	Das habe ich ihm angeboten.
anklicken	*to click*	Ich habe viele Fotos angeklickt.
anlassen	*to leave on*	Ich denke, was ich anlassen kann.
annehmen	*to accept*	Ich habe das Ergebnis angenommen.
aufbauen	*to establish*	Die Firma hat seit 1950 aufgebaut.
aufessen	*to eat up*	Du musst das alle aufessen.
auffallen	*to stand out*	Wir versuchen, nicht aufzufallen.
aufmachen	*to open*	Er hat seine Tasche aufgemacht.
aufpassen	*to watch out*	Bitte passen Sie für Tiere auf.
aufregen	*to get upset*	Bitte regst du sich nicht auf.
aufschlagen	*to open*	Könntest du den Kasten aufschlagen?
aufsteigen	*to climb steps*	Ich möchte immer aufsteigen als den Ausflug benutzen.
aufstellen	*to set up*	Ich stelle die Geräte auf.
aufziehen	*to raise*	Bitte zeihen Sie Ihre Bücher auf.
ausgeben	*to spend/output*	Er hat viel Geld ausgegeben.
auskennen	*to be familiar with*	Ich habe die Stadt gut ausgekannt.
ausleihen	*to lend*	Könntest du deinen Kugelschreiber mich ausleihen?
ausräumen	*to empty out*	Kannst du das Zimmer sofort ausräumen?
ausrichten	*to leave a message*	Ich habe für ihn eine Nachricht ausgerichtet.
ausruhen	*to relax*	Samstagabend möchte ich ausruhen.
ausschalten	*to turn off*	Ich schalte den Fernseher aus.

Verb	Meaning	Sample Sentence
aussehen	*to appear*	Ich kann gut erkennen, dass Gott hat vor mir ausgesehen.
aussprechen	*to pronounce*	Können Sie schwierige Wörter mit einem Kuli in dem Mund deutlich aussprechen?
aussuchen	*to select*	Bitte suchen Sie die richtige Lösung aus.
austauschen	*to trade*	Hast du die Kleidung ausgetauscht?
austeilen	*to distribute*	Wann teilen Sie die Bücher aus?
ausverkaufen	*to sell-out*	Was möchtest du dieses Jahr ausverkaufen?
ausziehen	*to take off shoes*	Bitte ziehen Sie aus und kommen Sie danach.
dazugehören	*to fit in*	Das Bild gehört an der Wand dazu.
durcheinandergehen	*to getmixed up*	Ich mache mich sorge, weil in meinem Kopf alle durcheinandergegangen ist.
einbauen	*to incorporate*	Haben Sie die Unterschiede eingebaut?
einfallen	*to think of*	Was fällst du seit einer Stunde ein?
eingeben	*to input*	Was möchten Sie diesem Computer eingeben?
eingehen	*to focus on*	Bitte gehen Sie auf Ihre Arbeit ein.
einhalten	*to follow/observe*	Wir müssen die Regeln einhalten.
einkochen	*to boil down*	Ich koche ein Ei ein.
einlenken	*to give in/back down*	Weil er nicht sicher war, bin ich auch eingelenkt.
einlösen	*to encash*	Bitte lösen Sie das Geld sofort ein.
einreiben	*to rub in*	Sein Auto hat leider eingerieben.
einschalten	*to turn on*	Ich schalte den Fernseher ein.
einsteigen	*to climb in*	Ich steige dem Bus ein.
einzeichnen	*to sketch*	Ich zeichne dich ein.
einziehen	*to move in*	Wir ziehen zu einer neuen Wohnung ein.
entlanggehen	*to go along*	Nach dem Rathaus gehen Sie den Fluss entlang.
fernsehen	*to see TV*	Wann möchten Sie vielleicht fernsehen?
feststellen	*to determine/discover*	Ich habe eine feststellen.
fortsetzen	*to continue*	Jetzt setzt das Gedicht fort.
freihaben	*to be free*	Sie müssen am Samstagabend für die Grillparty freihaben.
glattgehen	*to go smoothly*	Alles ist glattgegangen.
gutmachen	*to do well*	Er macht in der Prüfung gut.
herausnehmen	*to take out*	Bitte nehmen Sie Ihre Bücher heraus.
herumgehen	*to go around*	Sie müssen der Kirche herumgehen.
hineinlegen	*to insert*	Bitte legen Sie die DVD richtig hinein.
hineinschauen	*to look into*	Ich schaue sofort hinein.
hinfahren	*to drive to*	Er fährt nach Delhi hin.
hinsetzen	*to sit down*	Bitte setzen Sie sich hin.

Verb	Meaning	Sample Sentence
hinterlassen	*to leave behind*	Sie hat ihr Buch hinterlassen.
hochladen	*to upload*	Wie kann ich diese Information auf dem Internet hochladen?
kaputtgehen	*to fall apart*	Alles war kaputtgegangen, trotzdem bin ich hoffnungsvoll.
losgehen	*to start*	Das Konzert geht um 15:00 Uhr los.
mitlesen	*to read along*	Könnten wir das morgen mitlesen?
mitnehmen	*to take along*	Kann ich deinen Freund nach Bangalore mitnehmen?
nachdenken	*to ponder*	Woran denkst du nach?
nachfragen	*to ask again*	Bitte fühlen Sie frei, etwas nachzufragen.
rübergeben	*to pass over*	Ich gebe ihm das Buch rüber.
runterladen	*to download*	Gestern habe ich einen schönen Film runtergeladen.
stattfinden	*to take place*	Das Konzert findet am Samstagnachmittag statt.
teilnehmen	*to participate*	Möchten Sie in dem Sprachkurs teilnehmen?
überlegen	*to think over*	Haben Sie schon überlegt?
umdrehen	*to turn around*	Nach der Kirche drehen Sie links um.
umrühren	*to agitate*	Er umrührt sich über der Prüfung.
unternehmen	*to undertake*	Was nehmen Sie unter?
vorbeigehen	*to pass by*	Nach dem Rathaus gehen Sie den Fluss vorbei.
vorgehen	*to have precedence*	Wir müssen sicherlich vorgehen.
vorhaben	*to have planned*	Was haben Sie heute vor?
vorkommen	*to occur/happen*	Das Konzert ist letztes Jahr vorgekommen.
vorlesen	*to read aloud*	Sie müssen Deutsch immer genau vorlesen.
vorspielen	*to act out*	Ich spiele eine Rolle vor.
vortragen	*to recite/deliver*	Möchten Sie in der Präsentation etwas vertragen?
wegfahren	*to drive away*	Er fährt sofort weg.
weitergeben	*to pass on*	Er sollte die Informationen weitergeben.
weitergehen	*to go further*	Es ist schon Abend und ich meine, dass Sie nicht weitergehen dürfen.
weiterhelfen	*to assist*	Ich glaube, könntest du mir weiterhelfen?
weitermachen	*to continue*	Sie können nach der Pause die Reise weitermachen.
weiterschreiben	*to continue writing*	Bitte denken Sie klar und schreiben Sie dann weiter.
wiedergeben	*to reproduce*	Sie müssen in der Prüfung die Informationen wiedergeben.
wiederholen	*to revise*	Wir müssen immer wiederholen.
wohlfühlen	*to feel well*	Fühlen Sie heute wohl?
zuhaben	*to be closed*	Ich bin zurückgekommen, weil er die Geschäfte zugehabt hat.

Verb	Meaning	Sample Sentence
zukleben	*to seal*	Die Dokumente waren zugeklebt.
zumachen	*to close*	Ich mache meine Augen zu.
zunehmen	*to increase*	Können Sie die Musik zunehmen?
zurechtkommen	*to cope up*	Er kommt sofort mit dem Kurs zurecht.
zurückkommen	*to return*	Um wie viel Uhr kommen Sie zurück.
zurückrufen	*to call back*	Hast du mich nicht zurükruft?
zusammenfassen	*to summarize*	Bitte fassen Sie in zehn Minuten zusammen.
zusammengehören	*to fit together*	Sie Biden gehört richtig zusammen.
zustimmen	*to agree*	Stimmen Sie mit mir zu?

Appendix 8. List of Irregular Partizip II for A2

Infinitiv	Präsens	Präteritum	Partizip II
abschließen	er schließt ab	er schloss ab	hat abge**schloss**en
anbieten	er bietet an	er bot an	hat ange**bot**en
backen	er backt	er backte	hat gebacken
begraben	er begräbt	er begrub	hat begraben
benehmen	er benimmt	er benahm	hat be**nomm**en
besitzen	er besitzt	er besaß	hat be**sess**en
bestehen	er besteht	er bestand	hat bestanden
durcheinandergehen	er geht durcheinander	er ging durcheinander	ist durcheinandergegangen
einfallen	er fällt ein	er fiel ein	ist eingefallen
eingeben	er gibt ein	er gab ein	hat eingegeben
einhalten	er halt ein	er hielt ein	hat eingehalten
entlanggehen	er geht entlang	er ging entlang	ist entlanggegangen
entnehmen	er entnimmt	er entnahm	hat ent**nomm**en
entstehen	er entsteht	er entstand	ist ent**stand**en
entwerfen	er entwerft	er entwarf	hat ent**worf**en
erfinden	er erfindet	er erfand	hat er**fund**en
erhalten	er erhält	er erhielt	hat erhalten
erscheinen	er erscheint	er erschien	ist er**schie**nen
erschließen	er erschließt	er erschloss	hat erschlossen
erwachsen	er erwächst	er erwuchs	ist erwachsen
fließen	er fließt	er floss	ist ge**floss**en
gebären	er gabiert	er gebar	hat ge**bor**en
gelten	er gilt	er galt	hat ge**golt**en
gießen	er gießt	er goss	hat ge**goss**en
kaputtgehen	er geht kaputt	er ging kaputt	ist kaputtgegangen
leihen	er leiht	er lieh	hat geli**eh**en
lügen	er lügt	er log	hat ge**log**en
mitnehmen	er nimmt mit	er nahm mit	hat mit**genomm**en
nachdenken	er denkt nach	er dachte nach	hat nachge**dacht**
reiben	er reibt	er rieb	hat geri**eb**en
reiten	er reitet	er ritt	ist ge**ritt**en
rennen	er rennt	er rannte	ist ge**ran**nt
schießen	er schießt	er schoss	ist ge**schoss**en
springen	er springt	er sprang	ist ge**sprung**en
sterben	er stirbt	er starb	ist ge**storb**en
stinken	er stinkt	er stank	hat ge**stunk**en
streiten	er streitet	er stritt	hat ge**stritt**en
unterhalten	er unterhaltet	er unterhielt	hat unterhalten

Infinitiv	Präsens	Präteritum	Partizip II
überweisen	er überweist	er überwies	hat überwiesen
verbieten	er verbietet	er verbot	hat verboten
vergehen	er vergeht	er verging	ist vergangen
verlaufen	er verläuft	er verlief	ist verlaufen
verlieren	er verliert	er verlor	hat verloren
verschieben	er verschiebt	er verschob	hat verschoben
verschlafen	er verschläft	er verschlief	hat verschlafen
verschwinden	verschwindet	verschwand	ist verschwunden
versprechen	er verspricht	er versprach	hat versprochen
vertreten	er vertritt	er vertrat	ist vertreten
vorbeigehen	er geht vorbei	er ging vorbei	ist vorbeigegangen
vorlesen	er liest vor	er las vor	hat vorgelesen
vorschlagen	er schlägt vor	er schlug vor	hat vorgeschlagen
vortragen	er trägt vor	er trug vor	hat vorgetragen
wachsen	er wächst	er wuchs	ist gewachsen
weisen	er weist	er wies	hat gewiesen
weiterhelfen	er hilft weiter	er half weiter	hat weitergeholfen
werben	er wirbt	er warb	hat geworben
werfen	er wirfst	er warf	hat geworfen
zunehmen	er nimmt zu	er nahm zu	hat zugenommen
zurechtkommen	er kommt zurecht	er kam zurecht	ist zurechtgekommen

Appendix 9. List of Adjectives for A2

das Adjektiv und Gegenteil	Meaning	Komparativ	Superlativ
dicht X dünn	*dense*	dichter	am dichtesten
	slim	dünner	am dünnsten
gierig X großzügig	*stingy*	gieriger	am gierigsten
	generous	großzügiger	am großzügigsten
höflich X unhöflich	*polite*	höflicher	am höflichsten
	impolite	unhöflich	am unhöflichsten
hübsch X verrückt	*pretty*	hübscher	am hübschesten
	crazy	verrückt	am verrücktesten
praktisch X unpraktisch	*practical*	praktischer	am praktischsten
	impractical	unpraktischer	am unpraktischersten
sauber X schmutzig	*clean*	sauberer	am saubersten
	dirty	schmutziger	am schmutzigsten
scharf X süß	*spicy*	schärfer	am schärfsten
	sweet	süßer	am süßesten
sicher X unsicher	*certain*	sicherer	am sichersten
	uncertain	unsicherer	am unsichersten

Appendix 10. Groups of similar Verbs for A1 and A2

Learning new verbs in German should always be done with the conjugations in present tense, past tense and the Perfekt along with the Hilfsverb. An example using the verb **kommen** is as follows:

Infinitiv	Präsens	Präteritum	Perfekt
kommen	kommt	kam	ist gekommen

At A1 level, it is necessary to grab as many verbs as possible so that a strong foundation is built. Once the learner reaches the A2 level, certain similarities can be found among the verbs and groups of similar verbs with similar conjugation patterns can be made. This can be seen mainly in verbs that are irregular in the simple past or the present perfect tenses. Irregularity is generally grouped with reference to the formation of Partizip II. The Präteritum is not considered as it is used less often as compared to Perfekt. ollowing tables shall attempt to group such verbs with indicative explaEnations. The list is not limited although an attempt has been done to add all the verbs recommended for A1 and A2 levels.

Group 1: Irregular Präteritum and Partizip II has 'ge' attached to the infinitive
The Präteritum is generally irregular and needs to be memorized as there is a major change in the vowel or the complete spelling itself. Comparatively, the Partizip II is simple. It is formed by simply adding a **ge** to the verb infinitive. For verbs with separable prefixes, the **ge** is added between the sepeable prefix and the basic verb.

Infinitiv	Präsens	Präteritum	Perfekt
backen	er bäckt	er buk	hat gebacken
einfallen	er fällt ein	er fiel ein	ist eingefallen
eingeben	er gibt ein	er gab ein	hat eingegeben
einhalten	er halt ein	er hielt ein	hat eingehalten
einladen	er lädt ein	er lud ein	hat eingeladen
erhalten	er erhält	er erhielt	hat erhalten
fahren	er fährt	er fuhr	ist gefahren
fallen	er fällt	er fiel	ist gefallen
fangen	er fängt	er fing	hat gefangen
geben	er gibt	er gab	hat gegeben
halten	er hält	er hielt	hat gehalten
heißen	er heißt	er heiß	hat geheißen
kommen	er kommt	er kam	ist gekommen
laden	er lädt	er lud	hat geladen
lassen	er lässt	er ließ	hat gelassen
laufen	er läuft	er lief	ist gelaufen
lesen	er liest	er las	hat gelesen
raten	er rät	er riet	hat geraten
rufen	er ruft	er rief	hat gerufen
schlafen	er schläft	er schlief	hat geschlafen

Infinitiv	Präsens	Präteritum	Perfekt
schlagen	er schlägt	er schlug	hat geschlagen
sehen	er sieht	er sah	hat gesehen
tragen	er trägt	er trug	hat getragen
vorlesen	er liest vor	er las vor	hat vorgelesen
vorschlagen	er schlägt vor	er schlug vor	hat vorgeschlagen
vortragen	er trägt vor	er trug vor	hat vorgetragen
wachsen	er wächst	er wuchs	ist gewachsen

Group 2: Partizip II is same as the infinitive (verbs with or without inseperable prefix)

The Präteritum is generally irregular and needs to be memorized as there is a major change in the vowel or the complete spelling itself. The Partizip II is same as the verb infinitive.

Infinitiv	Präsens	Präteritum	Perfekt
begraben	er begräbt	er begrub	hat begraben
bekommen	er bekommt	er bekam	hat bekommen
erwachsen	er erwächst	er erwuchs	ist erwachsen
gefallen	er gefällt	er gefiel	hat gefallen
unterhalten	er unterhaltet	er unterhielt	hat unterhalten
vergessen	er vergisst	er vergaß	hat vergessen
verlaufen	er verläuft	er verlief	ist verlaufen
verraten	er verrät	er verriet	hat verraten
verschlafen	er verschläft	er verschlief	hat verschlafen
vertreten	er vertritt	er vertrat	ist vertreten

Group 3: Diphthong 'ie' in infinitive changes to 'ei' in Partizip II

There is a change in diphthongs in Präteritum and Partizip II forms from **ei** to **ie**

Infinitiv	Präsens	Präteritum	Perfekt
beschr**ei**ben	er beschreibt	er beschr**ie**b	hat beschr**ie**ben
bleiben	er bleibt	er blieb	ist geblieben
entscheiden	er entscheidet	er entschied	hat entschieden
erscheinen	er erscheint	er erschien	ist erschienen
leihen	er leiht	er lieh	hat geliehen
reiben	er reibt	er rieb	hat gerieben
scheinen	er scheint	er schien	hat geschienen
schreiben	er schreibt	er schrieb	hat geschrieben
schreien	er schreit	er schrie	hat geschrien
steigen	er steigt	er stieg	ist gestiegen
überweisen	er überweist	er überwies	hat überwiesen
vergleichen	er vergleicht	er verglich	hat vergliechen
weisen	er weist	er wies	hat gewiesen

Group 4: Letters ä, e, i, ü and diphthong 'ie' in infinitiv changes to 'o' in Partizip II

Letters and diphthongs in the infinitive in this group are generally replaced by **o** in Partizip II with the prefix **ge** added if the verb does not have an inseperable prefix

Infinitiv	Präsens	Präteritum	Perfekt
abschl**ie**ßen	er schließt ab	er schl**oss** ab	hat abgeschl**oss**en
anbieten	er bietet an	er bot an	hat angeboten
beginnen	er beginnt	er begann	hat begonnen
benehmen	er benimmt	er benahm	hat benommen
bewerben	er bewirbt	er bewarb	hat beworben
biegen	er biegt	er bog	hat gebogen
bieten	er bietet	er bot	hat geboten
empfehlen	er empfiehlt	er empfahl	hat empfohlen
entnehmen	er entnimmt	er entnahm	hat entnommen
entwerfen	er entwerft	er entwarf	hat entworfen
erschießen	er erschießt	er erschoss	hat erschossen
erschließen	er erschließt	er erschloss	hat erschlossen
fliegen	er fliegt	er flog	ist geflogen
fließen	er fließt	er floss	ist geflossen
gebären	er gabiert	er gebar	hat geboren
gelten	er gilt	er galt	hat gegolten
genießen	er genießt	er genoss	hat genossen
gewinnen	er gewinnt	er gewann	hat gewonnen
gießen	er gießt	er goss	hat gegossen
helfen	er hilft	er half	hat geholfen
lügen	er lügt	er log	hat gelogen
mitnehmen	er nimmt mit	er nahm mit	hat mitgenommen
nehmen	er nimmt	er nahm	hat genommen
riechen	er riecht	er roch	hat gerochen
schießen	er schießt	er schoss	ist geschossen
schließen	er schließt	er schloss	hat geschlossen
schwimmen	er schwimmt	er schwamm	ist geschwommen
sprechen	er spricht	er sprach	hat gesprochen
sterben	er stirbt	er starb	ist gestorben
treffen	er trifft	er traf	hat getroffen
verbieten	er verbietet	er verbot	hat verboten
verlieren	er verliert	er verlor	hat verloren
verschieben	er verschiebt	er verschob	hat verschoben
versprechen	er verspricht	er versprach	hat versprochen
weiterhelfen	er hilft weiter	er half weiter	hat weitergeholfen
werben	er wirbt	er warb	hat geworben
werden	er wird	er wurde	ist geworden
werfen	er wirfst	er warf	hat geworfen

wiegen	er wiegt	er wog	hat gewogen
ziehen	er zieht	er zog	ist gezogen
zunehmen	er nimmt zu	er nahm zu	hat zugenommen

Group 5: Letter 'i' in infinitiv changes to 'u' in Partizip II

The letter **i** in the infinitive form of the verb is generally replaced by **a** or **u** in Präteritum and **u** in the Partizip II

Infinitiv	Präsens	Präteritum	Perfekt
binden	er bindet	er band	hat gebunden
erfinden	er erfindet	er erfand	hat erfunden
finden	er findet	er fand	hat gefunden
klingen	er klingt	er klangt	hat geklungen
mißlingen	er mißlingt	er mißlang	ist mißlungen
springen	er springt	er sprang	ist gesprungen
stinken	er stinkt	er stank	hat gestunken
trinken	er trinkt	er trank	hat getrunken
verbinden	verbindet	er verband	hat verbunden
verschwinden	verschwindet	verschwand	ist verschwunden
wissen	er weiß	er wusste	hat gewusst

Group 6: Irregular change in vowel in Infinitiv and Partizip II

The vowel in the infinitive form changes to some other vowel in an irregular manner with no particular pattern. However, the Partizip II looks similar to the infinitive form with a few changes in its vowels and nearby letter(s). The Partizip II ends with **en** or **t** with **ge** added if the verb does not have an inseperable prefix.

Infinitiv	Präsens	Präteritum	Perfekt
bestehen	er besteht	er bestand	hat bestanden
bitten	er bittet	er bat	hat gebeten
bringen	er bringt	er brachte	hat gebracht
denken	er denkt	er dachte	hat gedacht
entstehen	er entsteht	er entstand	ist entstanden
erkennen	er erkennt	er erkannte	hat erkannt
kennen	er kennt	er kannte	hat gekannt
liegen	er liegt	er lag	hat gelegen
nachdenken	er denkt nach	er dachte nach	hat nachgedacht
nennen	er nennt	er nannte	hat genannt
reiten	er reitet	er ritt	ist geritten
rennen	er rennt	er rannte	ist gerannt
schneiden	er schneidet	er schnitt	hat geschnitten
stehen	er steht	er stand	ist gestanden
streichen	er streicht	er strich	ist gestrichen
streiten	er streitet	er stritt	hat gestritten

tun	er tut	er tat	hat getan
verstehen	er versteht	er verstand	hat verstanden

Group 7: Completely irregular and need to be memorized			

This last group has all such verbs that follow no particular pattern in formation of Partizip II. Certain verbs like **gehen** and **essen** are completely irregular in Präteritum and Perfekt and there is no particular pattern of formation of the same.

Infinitiv	Präsens	Präteritum	Perfekt
besitzen	er besitzt	er besaß	hat besessen
entlanggehen	er geht entlang	er ging entlang	ist entlanggegangen
essen	er isst	er aß	hat gegessen
gehen	er geht	er ging	ist gegangen
kaputtgehen	er geht kaputt	er ging kaputt	ist kaputtgegangen
mögen	er mag	er mochte	hat gemocht
sein	er ist	er war	ist gewesen
sitzen	er sitzt	er saß	hat gesessen
vergehen	er vergeht	er verging	ist vergangen
vorbeigehen	er geht vorbei	er ging vorbei	ist vorbeigegangen

Appendix 11. Summary of Articles for A2

This section summarizes all the different types of articles learnt for all the three genders in the Nominative, Accusative, Dative and the Genitive Cases.

die Unbestimmterartikeln – Nominativ, Akkusativ, Dativ und Genitiv

	maskulin	feminin	neutrum	plural
Nominativ	ein	eine	ein	-
Akkusativ	einen	eine	ein	-
Dativ	einem	einer	einem	-
Genitiv	eines	einer	eines	-

die Negationartikeln – Nominativ, Akkusativ, Dativ und Genitiv

	maskulin	feminin	neutrum	plural
Nominativ	kein	keine	kein	keine
Akkusativ	keinen	keine	kein	keine
Dativ	keinem	keiner	keinem	keinen
Genitiv	keines	keiner	keines	keiner

die Bestimmterartikeln – Nominativ, Akkusativ, Dativ und Genitiv

	maskulin	feminin	neutrum	plural
Nominativ	der	die	das	die
Akkusativ	den	die	das	die
Dativ	dem	der	dem	den
Genitiv	des	der	des	der

die Alleartikeln – Nominativ, Akkusativ, Dativ und Genitiv

		Unbestimmter	Negationsartikel	Bestimmter
maskulin	Nominativ	ein	kein	der
	Akkusativ	einen	keinen	den
	Dativ	einem	keinem	dem
	Genitiv	eines	keines	des
feminin	Nominativ	eine	keine	die
	Akkusativ	eine	keine	die
	Dativ	einer	keiner	der
	Genitiv	einer	keiner	der
neutrum	Nominativ	ein	kein	das
	Akkusativ	ein	kein	das
	Dativ	einem	keinem	dem
	Genitiv	eines	keines	des
plural	Nominativ	-	keine	die
	Akkusativ	-	keine	die
	Dativ	-	keinen	den
	Genitiv	-	keiner	der

Following tables indicate the possessive pronoun forms for all the four cases.

	Pronomen	maskulin	feminin	neutrum	plural
NOMINATIV	ich	mein	meine	mein	meine
	du	dein	deine	dein	deine
	er	sein	seine	sein	seine
	sie	ihr	ihre	ihr	ihre
	es	sein	seine	sein	seine
	wir	unser	unsere	unser	unsere
	ihr	eure	eure / euere	euer	eure / euere
	sie	ihr	ihre	ihr	ihre
	Sie	Ihr	Ihre	Ihr	Ihre

	Pronomen	maskulin	feminin	neutrum	plural
AKKUSATIV	ich	meinen	meine	mein	meine
	du	deinen	deine	dein	deine
	er	seinen	seine	sein	seine
	sie	ihren	ihre	ihr	ihre
	es	seinen	seine	sein	seine
	wir	unseren	unsere	unser	unsere
	ihr	euren	eure / euere	euer	eure / euere
	sie	ihren	ihre	ihr	ihre
	Sie	Ihren	Ihre	Ihr	Ihre

	Pronomen	maskulin	feminin	neutrum	plural
DATIV	ich	meinem	meiner	meinem	meinen
	du	deinem	deiner	deinem	deinen
	er	seinem	seiner	seinem	seinen
	sie	ihrem	ihrer	ihrem	ihren
	es	seinem	seiner	seinem	seinen
	wir	unserem	unserer	unserem	unseren
	ihr	eurem	euerer	eurem	euren
	sie	ihrem	ihrer	ihrem	ihren
	Sie	Ihrem	Ihrer	Ihrem	Ihren

<table>
<tr><td rowspan="10">GENITIV</td><td>Pronomen</td><td>maskulin</td><td>feminin</td><td>neutrum</td><td>plural</td></tr>
<tr><td>ich</td><td>meines</td><td>meiner</td><td>meines</td><td>meiner</td></tr>
<tr><td>du</td><td>deines</td><td>deiner</td><td>deines</td><td>deiner</td></tr>
<tr><td>er</td><td>seines</td><td>seiner</td><td>seines</td><td>seiner</td></tr>
<tr><td>sie</td><td>ihres</td><td>ihrer</td><td>ihres</td><td>ihrer</td></tr>
<tr><td>es</td><td>seines</td><td>seiner</td><td>seines</td><td>seiner</td></tr>
<tr><td>wir</td><td>unseres</td><td>unserer</td><td>unseres</td><td>unserer</td></tr>
<tr><td>ihr</td><td>eures</td><td>euerer</td><td>eures</td><td>euerer</td></tr>
<tr><td>sie</td><td>ihres</td><td>ihrer</td><td>ihres</td><td>ihrer</td></tr>
<tr><td>Sie</td><td>Ihres</td><td>Ihrer</td><td>Ihres</td><td>Ihrer</td></tr>
</table>

References

1. Netzwerk A2 Kursbuch, Arbeitsbuch and Glossary; 2015 Indian Edition, Langenscheidt, Printed and distributed in India by Goyal Publishers

2. NPTEL Course "German 2" of IIT Madras by Dr. Milind Brahme and Dr. Sashirekha Mannava

3. German in 30 days, Goyal Publishers, 2007 Edition

4. Youtube Videos on Channel: Learn German with Kedar Jadhav

5. Youtube Videos on Channel: Learn German with Anja

6. Youtube Videos on Channel: Your German Teacher

7. Official website of Goethe Institut

8. Let's Learn German A1, Gourav Vivek Kulkarni, Notion Press, October 2021, ISBN: 9781684875924

9. Other Internet resources